A FURNACE FULL OF GOD

Also by Rebekah Scott

The Moorish Whore

The Great Westward Walk
(translation)

A FURNACE FULL OF GOD

REBEKAH SCOTT

Peaceable Publishing

PEACEABLE PUBLISHING

ISBN: 978-0-9855032-2-2
First printing, 2019.

Some names and identifying details have been changed
in this book to protect the privacy of individuals.

Camino & Moratinos map illustrations: Jill Berry Design
Cover photograph: Kim Narenkivicius

*Peaceable Publishing, Moratinos, Palencia Spain
& Apollo, Pennsylvania USA*

www.peaceablekingdomcamino.com

For Paddy.

BAY OF BISCAY
SANTIAGO DE COMPOSTELA
SARRIA
PONFERRADA
LEON
BURGOS
PORTUGAL
MADRID
SPAIN
SEVILLE

CHAPTERS

CHAPTERS

FOREWORD

By George D. Greenia

Founder, Institute for Pilgrimage Studies, College of William & Mary

I first visited Santiago de Compostela, the goal of the Way of St. James, maybe thirty years ago. I was going to be in Spain that year and a good friend was running his university's study abroad program there. It was another Spanish city I had never visited. He offered me a free place to stay.

Only a few thousand pilgrims arrived in Santiago that year. I don't think I saw any of them. I'm not sure I looked.

News of the Camino de Santiago swelled through the 1990s, mostly fueled by reports of adventuresome foreigners who flooded onto its new recovered trails. The trek to Santiago drew the historically curious, hikers who were not campers, nature lovers, and gentle believers who were not required to present sober Catholic credentials. Unlike Lourdes and Fatima where miracles had occurred and participating in devotions was the whole point of the trip, Santiago asked for a communal journey. The processions were not in plazas or from church to church. They were open-air, and could take weeks or months. It was Mecca on the meseta.

I met Rebekah Scott soon after my own first trek. I started out bicycling strenuous distances to "earn" Santiago: from Paris, about 1200 miles away, and a round trip from Salamanca, about 800. Rebekah confirmed my growing intuition that biking was a self-defeating shortcut. I was visiting the shrines, sampling the weather and landscapes, but shunning the community. The walkers were mysterious, churning the footpaths in calm silence. Could I earn being one of them?

My first walk changed me. I never intended to make it to Santiago. I only had a few weeks, enough to walk from Roncesvalles on the Spanish side of the Pyrenees, down the crumpled foothills toward Pamplona, through windy Navarrese wheat fields and orderly Riojan vineyards as far as Burgos. Beyond there start the tablelands where the planet itself slopes away on every side and the Spanish ruefully affirm that "your landscape is the sky."

I never bicycled again.

My dozen Caminos since those early staggering forays into the air have always been on foot among fellow walkers. If I earned my place among them, it was by listening to their stories.

And the best archive of pilgrim stories I ever tapped into was the one carried with such effortless grace by Rebekah Scott.

This book is a clean arc of tales brought by strangers and told in a night. It is also the theater of storytelling itself, the hardscrabble village on the meseta where pilgrims come to eat and sleep and allow their stories to pool. It is even the story of those who will never walk, who cannot walk, who patiently host those who come to recite their dreams and disappear.

Rebekah and I are married to men who understand how our companionship enriches us and who encourage us to walk without them. I listen to her stories, I try to tell a few of my own. We sit with pilgrim strangers who are full of wit, and snark, and weariness of life, and sometimes holy insight. We value what we learn from each. They mistake us for lovers, or researchers, or religious out of habit. We are just pilgrims like they are.

The stories in this book are those of the village on the meseta where Rebekah and her husband have made their home for over a decade. Pilgrims and neighbors arrive, are sheltered and fed, leave their stories as their coin of gratitude.

This book will fill your backpack with the same coin for your journey.

Williamsburg, Virginia USA
March 2019

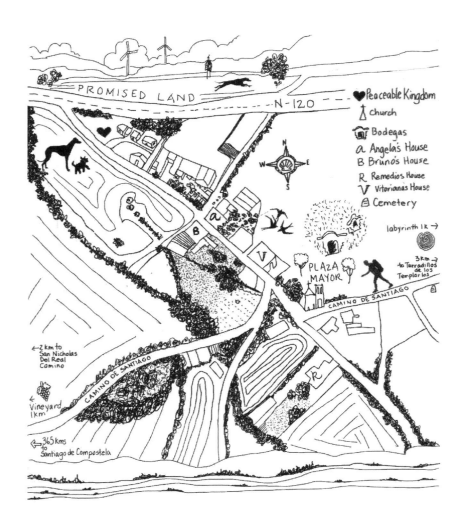

PROMISED LAND ———— N-120

♥ Peaceable Kingdom
♈ Church
🏠 Bodegas
α Angela's House
B Bruno's House
R Remedios House
V Vitorianas House
🏛 Cemetery

N
W ✦ E
S

labyrinth 1k →

3km
to Terradillos
de los
Templarios

PLAZA
MAYOR

CAMINO DE SANTIAGO

← 2 km to
San Nicholas
Del Real
Camino

CAMINO DE SANTIAGO

←
Vineyard
1km

← 365 kms
to
Santiago de Compostela

MORATINOS

PROMISED LAND
JULY 2018

It takes a good two hours to walk the whole way around the Promised Land, and the black clouds were way over on the edge of the western horizon. We let the dogs off their leads. The sky is huge here, and the land below is a great rug of rolling fields, horizon to horizon. There's a sprinkling of villages, and wind turbines along the ridges, and a string of dark mountains to the north. This is the Meseta, the high-altitude prairie in the heart of Spain. We live in a sparsely-populated part called Palencia, where the thunderstorms and wind are particularly fierce. There is nothing here to slow them down.

The breeze blew westward, pushing the storm away from us. The dogs, Judy and Ruby, ran full-out into a wide field of garish sunflowers.

The storm was moving off. Paddy said we'd make it home with no trouble.

Up the rutted tractor path a kilometer or two, then around the curve. The wind shifted. The black cloud lumbered back. It filled up half the sky with layers of boiling dark blue and grey. It reached its great hand over us. Lightning! Lightning! I counted the seconds up to the thunder. The storm was immense, but still three or four kilometers away.

"If I saw that in a painting, I'd say it was overdone," Paddy said. "Vulgar, even."

"Come on, Pad. Let's move," I said.

The breeze shushed and crackled through the acres of dry ripe rye. It picked dust up off the ruts and sent it swirling up the road. A lark ascended, reeling out her song like a wind-up toy. Ruby Dog trotted ahead, her head turned to the right, watching the storm take over. The front of the cloud touched the ground and went hazy with rain. We were on the last stretch home. We still had a ways to go.

"Fifteen minutes, maybe, and we'll be there," Paddy said. Thunder rumbled hard. Three hawks circled round the face of the black cloud. Three crows called out from the ground. The larks sang on, oblivious. To the east the sky was clear and bright blue. It was cinematic.

"We might get wet," I said. "I can run ahead, get the dogs home, get the car, come back for you."

"Why would you do that?"

"I don't want lightning to strike you."

"That is extremely unlikely," Paddy said. "Slow down. Walk with me. Don't leave me out here."

Paddy walks a good five or six kilometers every morning, but he cannot move very fast any more. He walks with a stick. He's walked with a stick for five years now, but speeding up makes him cough. When he starts coughing, he goes all blank in the face, and can't stop. He's a healthy man, but for that.

Still, one morning last fall when his legs went weak, I left Pad out in the Promised Land. I went to get the car, but I did not leave him alone. Harry Dog stayed with him. I took the other dogs with me that time, put them in the barn, grabbed the keys and drove over the highway bridge and back into the great expanse. I picked up Paddy and Harry. All was well.

The next day, the doctor couldn't say why Paddy's legs did that. All his parts checked out just fine. "You're 76 years old," is all he could tell him. "Take it easy. Don't walk so far."

We don't usually walk so far nowadays, but the morning was so cool and breezy, more May than July. We should have taken the rightward fork, the shorter route.

I slowed down. I resigned myself to a good soaking. The rain wouldn't kill me.

The lightning could, though. Judy Dog came alongside and let herself be caught. If the bolt came down now, we'd all be fried together. Paddy, Judy, Ruby and me, called to glory from the Promised Land. A lot worse things could happen to us. We'd get our names in the paper for sure, and not just the obituary page.

Maybe we shouldn't walk out so often over at the P. L., beautiful as it is. Things happen out there. It is so wide-open, we are so small. Things tend to slip away into the air and the earth, sometimes things we love. Mostly dogs.

In our twelve years living on the Meseta, we've had a procession of stray dogs and cats come and stay and love and be loved – they are why we called our house "Peaceable Kingdom." All the dogs are walked out in the Promised Land. A lot of wild animals live in those ditches and draws. Over the years we've met up with foxes, deer, weasels, owls, hares, rabbits and thousands of field mice. The outcomes are bloody sometimes.

We give them the best care, but our animals do not live to great ages. They run into the road, they eat poisoned mice, they get cancer, or meet a fox or a bustard, or someone leaves a gate open and they run away into forever. Like Harry did, just this spring. Harry was a greyhound growing old, there was something wrong with his heart, and he ran away after a roe deer one morning, out in the Promised Land, wearing his bright red coat. We did not see him again.

Outside our back gate is a row of dog and cat graves, but some of the best beloved are not buried there. They knew their time was done, and they took themselves off. I believe they crossed the N-120 and headed over the highway bridge to the Promised Land. Una did it, when she felt the cancer closing in. Lulu, too, and Harry. Momo and Norman, cats, characters. All vanished, in their turns, without a trace.

I am a romantic, a believer. I like to think I'm tough and practical and down-to-earth, but I love drama and stories and miracles as much as anybody. Paddy's even more so – he's the one who started naming parts of our Plain-Jane landscape things like Grand Canyon, Lonesome Valley, and Roman Villa. We live near to the ground. We have to find our drama in the dirt, among the rye and oats, crows and adobe. And the sky. Clouds in the day, stars at night.

And in Tuesday-morning thunderstorms. The lightning didn't strike us dead, it didn't even strike anywhere near us. Paddy was not left behind in the downpour. We made it home just as the first dime-size drops hit the ground.

Paddy was right. He fed the dogs, and went to lie down. The rain pounded down for hours. It made the house cozy. The air smelled like fresh dirt.

I peeked into the darkened bedroom and saw Paddy stretched out on his side on the bed. I watched in the semi-dark until I saw that he was breathing. He's been telling me he's dying since I met him. He's a drama queen, in a cranky old man sort of way. One of these days, it will be for real.

Our early days were a headlong stride into a bright future, lots of trips and plans and chatter. We bushwhacked across the fields, hiked with our pack of dogs all along the ridges and draws of the Promised Land, all the way up to the bases of the windmills.

Now we take it day by day. Short walks to Pablo's Vineyard, out to the Neolithic Tomb, or over to San Nicolas for a coffee outside the pilgrim albergue. Six kilometers, max, then home again.

Home is a two-story adobe farmstead painted ochre yellow, tucked against a hillside. It sits at the topside of Moratinos, a tiny pueblo on the wide, high-altitude plain of Castile. A two-lane national road runs right outside our back gate, but almost nobody uses that old road any more. The European Union laid down a big Autopista a few dozen yards farther north. Beyond that, over the highway bridge, lies the Promised Land. We are lucky. There's a little hill between us and the highway. We get all the access and none of the noise.

We came here out of the noise of the United States, the stress of careers in daily journalism. It was a shock, but a welcome one, like diving into the deep end of the pool on an August afternoon. The shock as the water closes around your body, the flash of panic, blue-green chlorine clarity. Eight feet deep in silence. For a wonderful moment, you are a fish.

There is a great deal of that cool stillness in our house, a quiet sometimes so profound that visitors cannot sleep at night.

We've had visitors here since we arrived. Many of them

are pilgrims. Moratinos is a village on the pilgrim trail to Santiago de Compostela. For our first five years, our house was the only place in town where passers-by could stop and stay. We made them welcome. We'd chosen to live in a backwater, but people from all over the world travel the trail, and they kept things fresh for us. Some of them helped us renovate our house. Others sang for us, translated legal documents, reassured us, or did disastrous things meant to make our computers run better. We enjoyed most of them.

Pilgrims helped us paint our house yellow, so it blends into the yellow-brown ground around it. Ochre paint is cheap. It comes in pre-mixed buckets at the hardware store. White paint is cheapest of all, so that is the color of all the other houses in town. There are 24 houses in Moratinos. Ten of them have year-round residents. Most of the rest are open only in summer, when the faraway sons and daughters come back for the homecoming fiesta. A few more are abandoned, falling slowly back into the earth behind hand-written "Se Vende" for-sale signs.

Nobody buys adobe houses. Most of the old ones now are beyond hope. The roofs are failing, the walls are sagging. When they are gone, we will not see their like again. Adobes are too hard to care for, too dark and low. It's easier just to knock them down and put up something new.

The people here are not sentimental. This is a hard, real place that demands a lot of the people who stay here. It is a harsh prairie beauty, a Cistercian mix of silence and light and wind. People do not come here to retire, or to take holidays. Like Angela said, the very day we met, "This is not a place people come to. It is a place to escape from."

We've already done our leaving. We are done with America, and England. We plotted and planned this move for years, and when Moratinos made us welcome, we worked hard to fit in, to make them like us.

It would've been enough to just pay our bills on time, and show up at the Mass on Sunday morning. But when someone asked us over for coffee, we brought along a homemade zucchini bread. And a camera. I took pictures of everything then, and I posted them on a blog. I dug in, fascinated by the everyday, everything was so fresh and unknown, exciting – a bit like falling in love. And for the most part, Moratinos loved us back.

1

DEATH ON THE PATIO
2010

It was the first day of 2010, just after lunchtime. I was not invited to the throat-cutting, but I heard the screams from up the street.

I stepped into Vitoriana's patio just in time to see the pig come out of the fire. It was a sow, her two rows of teats burnt black. She stank with a greasy stink I'd never smelled before. The men moved her like cargo, stretched her out on an ancient wooden bench, and spread open her legs obscenely. With Neolithic-looking curls of steel they worked over her blackened skin, shaving off bristles and hair and char. A little boy was there, Alejandro was his name, about four years old. He pulled off a mitten and touched her carefully with the very tips of his fingers: her teats. Her black nose, dripping red. Her trotters, pliant, one by one.

Old Arturo picked up a sharpened steel triangle. He touched it to her throat. He took a breath, sank a corner in and drew the blade down the hog, halving her from chin to tail. She offered up her insides. Arturo unpacked each organ from the neat assortment: Bowels large and small. Bladder, lungs, liver, kidneys, heart. Juan and Carlos, Arturo's sons, circled the work in careful choreography. At just the right moment they handed in a bowl for the gall, traded a black-handled knife for the battered bit of steel. Arturo leaned into the labor, dividing and cleaving, hacking and pulling things free. His sons and brothers-in-law parted the pieces and hung them from hooks and rods in the rafters. The meat steamed. I was revolted, and fascinated. Butchering hogs is part of village life all over the world, and has been for centuries, millennia even. The family knew I was interested in these rural events, so they invited me over. I tried not to get underfoot.

Her insides emptied, hoisted upside-down and hooked to a beam, the sow changed from pig to pork. Her skin was sliced free from the fat beneath, her bones cracked apart with a hatchet, her joints undone. Arturo opened her wide as a dictionary, and Juan wedged a board inside her ribs to expose the meat to the cold. Tio Enrique splashed the carcass with water, then emptied the bucket onto the guttering fire.

We went inside and warmed our stinging hands at the coal stove. The men washed up, stripped off their coveralls and headed to the bar in San Nicolas. Mariluz and Remedios, Lucia and Raquel tied on their aprons and took up their stations at a long dining table. They stretched and soaked and carefully washed the intestines, the first step in the long road to sausages. By the end of the weekend most of the meat would be ground-up, spiced, and forced into the pig's own tubes to make great loops of chorizo and morcilla.

"Matanzas," pig-butcherings, are dying out in northern Spain. Only two of Moratinos' families raised a hog that year, and the first hard freeze spelled doom for the pigs. Butchering is best done when the temperature is low, so the meat can hang outdoors without going bad or attracting flies. It's a big job, killing and cutting-up such a large animal. It requires many hands working together.

The burnt-bristle stink lingered through the afternoon. The carcass dripped and steamed in the cold patio. Remedios hustled me into the kitchen and put me to work stirring a pot of thick inky juice over a very low flame.

"Go to the bathroom and have a pee first, because once you start this you can't stop," she said. "Don't let it boil. It's like making coffee... slow and steady. Keep it moving until I come for it. I'll turn on the TV here if you want. I know it's boring."

"No, no TV, it's not that bad," I said. "I can do this."

She left me, joined her sisters and nieces working and chattering in the next room, a big, low space where their father and grandfather once kept Moratinos' only store and tavern. I didn't mind being left in the kitchen. After an hour of butchery and rapid-fire Spanish I was ready for some peace. I didn't feel alone.

I stirred and stared into the fire. I remembered Vitoriana, Remedios' mother, who'd spent many years of her long life at this hearth. Vitoriana died a couple of years after we arrived. What would that old lady make of this foreigner in her kitchen?

I did not think she would mind. She knew me, after all, as much as she knew anyone toward the last of her ninety-six years. The first year I came she knew my name. For another year she thought I was her sister, come to visit – she asked me what I'd done to my hair. The summer after that she took to her narrow bed in the next room. Finally, she turned her gaze to the wall and quietly died.

Another year on, no one lived in Vitoriana's rambling house on the plaza corner, but her eight children joined together to maintain it. On holiday weekends, and through the summer they drove in from Burgos, Vittoria, and Madrid. They packed themselves and their children and grandchildren tight into the tiny, low rooms where they'd grown up. These people love company. They don't mind close quarters, especially if it's family. Especially if it's in their pueblo – their beloved, neglected, depopulated home village. Every self-respecting Spaniard has a pueblo, and he misses it fiercely, even if he hasn't been there for years.

Stirring the pot was a job for a child, but Alejandro was down for his nap and I was the least useful adult in the place. I used to bristle when anyone patronized me, but I've learned to take that in my stride. The ladies were right, and kind, to take special care of me. I didn't know a thing about butchering hogs or spicing sausages.

An hour later Remedios come for the pot. The inky stuff inside was the pig's blood, she said. A key ingredient in morcilla, a spicy, dense black sausage.

It was my turn to make dinner, back at home. I said my goodbyes. I thanked the ladies for inviting me, wished them a "Feliz Año."

"Thank you for helping," Mariluz said. "Come back tomorrow afternoon, we'll show you how to make chorizos."

I walked back up Calle Ontanon in the watery light of dusk, picking spots of dried blood off my sleeves. I thought about home.

It was late morning back in Pittsburgh. If I still was there I would have just finished the first round of calls to policemen, magistrates, emergency dispatchers, and started writing-up the mayhem of the night before for the daily newspaper.

New Year's Eve, lots of carnage. But no matanza. I was the only person I knew who'd help butcher a hog that day.

I love western Pennsylvania, but I am glad to be gone from there.

There, meat comes packaged in plastic. Pork has little to do with actual pigs. Death is a lofty concept best left to specialists. Some men still hunt deer, and some families, like mine, eat venison right through winter.

My father and his brothers hunted deer with the winter's first snowfall, like many Appalachian men. My father had no sons to hunt with him. His three daughters learned to shoot targets with a .22 rifle, but it was a rare girl who went into the woods to hunt. We saw plenty of game, but we never learned to gut and clean a carcass.

Men dealt death. Women roasted the venison, stewed the rabbit, fried the trout, set the table and served. When someone found a shotgun pellet in his pheasant, it was the cook who apologized, not the shooter.

I had seen creatures die before. I saw my first animal sacrifice at age 9, out behind our apartment building in Izmir, Turkey.

We were a military family on a three-year NATO posting. My father was a friendly man, and had forged a tie with Mehmet, the janitor in our low-rise apartment building. Mehmet and a few neighbors pooled their money and bought a ram to sacrifice at the end of each Ramadan season. The first year, we foreigners looked-on from our first-floor balcony as the ritual played out in the flower-bed below. My mother held my hand. She'd read to us the "Ramadan" entry from the encyclopedia, and assured us the priest was a professional butcher, like the Israelite high priests in the Old Testament. The ram wouldn't suffer. I squeezed shut my eyes at the fatal moment.

The second year I visited the scrawny sacrifice beforehand. I fed him raisins and felt his horns and wool. When the man with the knives arrived I stood well away, but I didn't leave. I watched. I saw the ram's eyes as he kicked and bled, faded, and died. It was not painless, but did not take long.

I've only ever killed one animal myself. I was 12, the victim was a duck, raised for a Thanksgiving Day feast back home in Pennsylvania. My cousin Barbara, a wiry woman with a great knowledge of practicalities, demonstrated first on a rooster. She then handed me the hatchet, and held down the tame, trusting duck while I made the fatal swing. After a wild bout of flapping and spattering, Barbara picked up the carcasses and showed me how to pluck, draw and bard them for roasting. I learned that healthy ducks have neon-yellow intestines, and their guts are suspended in a gelid glove of fat – fat that adds delicious richness to other foods. I liked learning those things.

But the killing disgusted me. I promised myself to never do that again. I loved Barbara like a child loves her best teacher, but I saw early on I wasn't cut out for full-on country life. I scrubbed my hands that day with carbolic soap. I knew that butchering ducks wasn't wrong, but I asked the Lord to forgive me anyway.

Barbara wasn't religious, but she was a Zen master, a matter-of-fact doer of deeds. She dug miles of post-holes and stretched wire for electric fences. She drove steam-rollers and forklifts at the nuclear power plant in Homer City, and welded radiators in her father's repair shop. There might be an orphan lamb or injured swan asleep in her bathtub, or a crate of Afghan Hound pups making messes in the living room. She kept an ugly snub-nosed .32 under the seat of her Jeep, was deeply suspicious of "colored people." When I said that was offensive, she said I'd spent too long with my nose in a book.

My cousin did more than her share of suffering. She'd lost a child to SIDS, and her home to an abusive ex. When her dad shot himself to death, Barb found his body.

Barb was not a great housekeeper or model citizen, but she had a profound influence on her gawky, lonely young cousin.

She taught me to handle horses, dogs, goats, and fowl; how to use a winch, a cinch, a corkscrew and a half-hitch knot; how to put a Jeep into four-wheel drive, open a lobster, down a shot of bourbon, slow down into a curve and accelerate out. She showed me how to butcher fowl, and gently teased me ever after for "turning green."

"Nothing you learn is ever wasted," she told me one day as we twisted baling-twine into hackamore halters and set out into the woods to bring in three half-wild horses. "You watch. This seems goofy, what we're doing here. But one day, you're going to remember this and say 'Yeah. I done this before. I know how.'"

I wanted to be like Barbara, even after I grew up. Someday, I told myself, I'll have an animal farm of my own, a barn, a garden, a box of good tools. I'll work hard, I will know how. I won't have to ask someone else to make it work for me.

It's because of Barb I pick up trash and broken creatures and people lying along the road. When I sickle down high weeds without chopping off my fingers, when I figure out some clever way to keep the chicken-house door closed, and when I tell a creep to "fuck off" without blushing with shame, I say a quiet thank-you to my cousin. She showed me how.

In 2006, when we decided to move to Spain, Barbara kept our dog Una at her house for the summer. That was the summer we found Moratinos, and bought our house. Barb would have loved our house, our village, our gang of animals. But Barb, by then, had terminal cancer. She did not live to see it.

When I sat by the fire, stirring pig's blood with Vitoriana's ghost, I think my cousin Barbara pulled up a stool, too.

That afternoon was years ago. Remedios' family hasn't had a matanza since. Too much trouble, feeding a piglet for so long, getting all those people together, getting the veterinary certificate. Only Segundino's family still butchers hogs, and they've never asked me to their matanza. I don't think I mind too much.

I want them to keep happening. I just don't want to be there to see it.

2

THE WELCOME BUSINESS

We have good neighbors, but we do not have close friends nearby. There is no expat community here. We don't play cards. We can't talk about the wholesale price of soybeans and barley, not with any confidence. We don't have a television, and our Spanish skills, even after so many years, are less than they should be. It's hard to talk for any length of time. We don't have a lot in common.

Animals are so much easier. They seem to understand what we say to them, and they never laugh at our verb choices. They don't smell good, but a lot of people stink, too. We don't have to go looking for animals. They have a way of finding us.

The greyhounds, for instance. The first two. We found them along the road one wintry morning soon after the matanza.

Una Dog spotted them first. She ran at them, pulled the lead from my hand, tore across two empty lanes of the N-120 and onto the dreary no-man's land between the on-ramp and the autopista. She wagged and yipped at the bottom of the steep bank, her bark bounced around the mouth of a big drainage pipe. Something moved in there, just beyond her.

I prayed it was not a fox. Two faces emerged from the dark. Four Egyptian eyes. Eyeliner eyes, full of fear. Dog faces, elegant and pointy.

Damn, I thought. Two dogs, big ones. I already have two dogs. We don't need more dogs.

But we couldn't just leave them in there. I scrabbled down the bank. They shrank away, crouching in ankle-deep water. Greyhounds. The Spanish kind – galgos. There was nowhere for them to go. They were barely standing up.

I whipped off my belt and slopped into the ditch. Icy water spilled into my boot-tops. I spoke quietly. Una wagged, enjoying the drama. I grabbed her lead. I reached out to the nearest hound. "You're a pretty one," I told her, reaching forward, the belt looped inside my hand. "Please don't bite me."

She stretched out her nose to sniff my hand. I slipped my belt over her head and 'round her neck. I asked her to come out. She tottered into the light. She was a spectacular brindle, brown with tiger stripes. The other galgo, spindly and ghostly-grey, followed close behind her, out of reach but not willing to be left behind. Slowly, quietly we crossed back over the road. Una pranced.

Over the road, Paddy and Tim waited to see what the rumpus was. Tim wagged his stumpy tail. Patrick's mouth made a silent O of surprise. He hunkered down to see the skeletal dogs at their level. They ducked behind me, shivering.

"Must be the greyhounds Kim saw," Patrick said softly. He took Una's lead.

"It's hare season. They must not have made the cut. The hunters must've dumped them," I said.

"How could they?" Patrick said in a whisper. The shy grey dog touched Patrick's hand with her nose. "They're beautiful," he said.

"Don't get attached. They're in bad shape," I said. "I think the gray one might not make it." We walked through the fog toward home. We spoke low, trying to sound grave, trying to keep excitement from our voices.

"These guys have to belong to someone. They might be valuable hunting dogs. I don't think they make good pets," I said.

My feet were frozen, my shoes sloshed with ditch-water. We crossed the fallow field, dropped down the path alongside the rosemary hedge and to our front gate. Hunched on the doorstep were two shaggy young men, assembling roll-up cigarettes.

"We are pilgrims," one of them said. A German. "We've got no money. The neighbors say you'll let us stay. We'll do chores if you need help."

I told them to come inside. Paddy took the dogs into the barn.

"You speak English?" the second man asked. A Scot, judging from the accent.

"I'm American. My husband is English," I said. "Rebekah. Patrick. If you're going to smoke, please do it outside." I looked each one in the eye and shook their hands. They tucked their cigarettes behind their ears and picked up their rucksacks.

"What are you doing living out here?" the Scot asked, incredulous. "Why this place?"

Everybody who comes here asks that. It's like clockwork. Every single one.

Fat raindrops splatted down. I showed the pilgrims to the Salon, the pilgrims' bedroom. Kim, a 30-something pilgrim who often stayed with us, greeted them, showed them the bathroom, and put the kettle on the stove.

"Leave that to me," I told her. "Go out to the barn. Paddy needs some help with the dogs."

From the patio I heard her cry of joy.

The galgos took up the rest of our day. In the kitchen we stroked their shivery suede hides with our open hands, to get them used to being touched. They were females, quite young, with notches cut in their ears. No collars or tattoos, no tags.

A chain was welded onto the neck of the shy grey. It cut into her skin.

They wolfed down kibble and water. They coiled up together on the warm spot in front of the sink, a malodorous heap of elbows, toes, and noses. Kim said she thought she'd seen them bounding through the misty fields, but perhaps she'd only dreamed them. And now they'd manifested!

The two pilgrims stacked firewood out back and hauled in enough for the night. They washed their clothes and bodies, and helped us eat pasta. They hung up their laundry to dry on the lines near the wood stove, and by 9:30 p.m. they were fast asleep.

The galgos slept, too. They slept for two days. I phoned the Guardia Civil. The dogs belonged to nobody. They were ours, the policeman said, congratulations! We already had two dogs inside the house, so we put the greyhounds in the barn to live. They seemed more comfortable there.

Word spread through the town. Carlos came over with bolt-cutters and snipped the chain from the grey girl's neck. Like most of the neighbors, Carlos loves to give advice.

"Galgos are not like regular dogs," he said, speaking slowly. "They're out-in-the-open wild animals. Once these two put on some weight, they'll run down and kill anything that moves. Like little dogs. Your cat. Your chickens.

And out in the field they'll kill the quails and rabbits. They can't help themselves. You'll have to be really careful," he warned. "Keeping galgos is more like keeping gazelles than dogs. To keep them like pets is foolishness."

We were fools. Our foreign habits made us the comic relief of Moratinos. We tried hard to fit in, and we asked a lot of odd questions. We found our function by dealing with the pilgrims, passers-by whom the neighbors viewed as fractionally more welcome than locusts. We were shown a lot of mercy, probably because we were child-like in our ignorance. Spaniards adore children.

Our foolishness had much to do with animals. I like animals, and Patrick loves them. When we moved to Spain we'd sought out a big house in the country with a patio, barn, and plenty of room for critters to run.

We brought Una, a scruffy terrier mutt, all the way from Pittsburgh. A few months after we arrived, a Brittany spaniel wandered away from the hunt and took up with some pilgrims. Twenty kilometers later they arrived at our house. The pilgrims moved on, but the spaniel stayed. We called him Tim.

Murphy was a kitten when he jumped out of a ditch and climbed up my pants-leg. I took him home. He grew into a magnificent barn cat, with cool green eyes and elegant pin-stripe pants.

Bob the Canary was named for Bob Dylan, but he turned out to be a much better singer. He filled up our kitchen with deafening music. Out back in a ramshackle pen were seven egg-laying hens and Max, a big bully rooster. (We'd tried out a donkey, but that ended in tears.) And so we had the little farm I'd dreamed of. None but the hens was particularly useful, but each one had a part in making our house a welcoming place.

We were in the welcoming business, and I suppose we still are. We live on a pilgrim trail, but for our first five years there was no bar, restaurant, store, or pilgrim shelter in Moratinos. The neighbors sent all inquirers over to our place. Some stayed for a coffee or a meal, others sheltered overnight. In the early days they slept on a mattress on the kitchen floor, or in unfinished bedrooms with rain dripping through the roof, or mice running along the baseboards, or hens cackling down the hallway. We didn't charge them anything to stay, but we often asked for a hand with the housework. There was a donation box by the front door.

Patrick and I had been pilgrims ourselves, and later "hospitaleros," volunteer hosts. We believe in pilgrimage. Pilgrims were the reason why we moved to a dying town on the prairie. Paddy was 69 when we left the United States. I was 48. We were retired, but we weren't old enough yet to sit still. In Moratinos, we could be useful, between bouts of idleness.

Pilgrims were our priority, but back then, few pilgrims traveled in winter. Northern Spain is cold and windy in winter, and most of the pilgrim hostels closed through the cold months. The few that opened on our stretch of prairie wouldn't turn on the heat without an extra five-euro "donation." Pilgrims are notoriously tight-fisted.

Winter pilgrims are hardcore. Most are men, walking to fulfill a promise made to God, or to work through a tough decision or life crisis. They walk many miles with wind and rain blowing into their faces, alone with their thoughts, with no one to talk to. Once they're shown a bed and showered and full of hot tea or red wine, most of them have good stories to tell. I love stories. That's one reason I love pilgrims, especially winter pilgrims. If you're walking 500 miles across a country in the rain, you may well be extraordinary.

Kim came to us in late winter, a wandering soul from Key West, Florida, walking the Camino in a years-long search for herself. She was a filmmaker, a graphic artist, born in Colorado and hauled like a papoose on her daddy's back to hear Jimi Hendrix play at Woodstock. Kim was in love with Spain, but spoke little Spanish. She'd spent some weeks at a collective farm in Bierzo, where latter-day hippies tend to fetch up. Someone told her about the English people at Moratinos. She looked us up. I remember.

It was a blindingly bright afternoon in March, 2009. I always get restless that time of year, and I was trailblazing, following the Camino San Salvador over a high mountain peak, making notes for an English-language trail guide.

I was alone on the side of a mountain, and I was in a jam.

Just over halfway to where I was going, the trail vanished into hip-deep snow. The faded yellow-arrow trail markers were buried. I wasn't sure if I was going the right way, and I had only four hours left of daylight. There was no telephone signal, and there was no real GPS in those days. I couldn't call down to the little mountain lodge at Pobladura for advice. Should I turn around and follow my footprints back, or move on into God-knows-what?

I wasn't afraid. The weather was clear. I knew how to get back to safety, but I really didn't want to backtrack. I was enjoying myself.

I sat down in the snow and inhaled. I pulled out my map and compass and took a hard look at the landscape. I was on the lip of a wide mountain valley, with a succession of white peaks marching away to the west like pioneers. I let myself sit there for a moment, soaking up the perfect silence. It was one of the most beautiful places I'd ever been.

I found where I was on the contour map, saw the little knoll in the rocks ahead where the trail ought to be. Four hours until sundown. I felt good. I would make it to Puerto de Pajares, I decided. I folded up the map, tucked it inside my coat. I gave thanks to the Girl Scouts of America for teaching me to find my way. I pulled myself upright, snow squeaking underfoot.

A musical phrase sang out into the mountain fastness. My mobile phone. It wasn't supposed to work up there!

It was a woman, an American. Her name was Kim. Words tumbled out like she hadn't spoken English for a while. "Can I come and stay at your house? I'll work for room and board," she said. "I love animals. I'm a good cook. I'll be quiet, I won't be a bother, you'll hardly know I'm there!"

A breeze picked up snow and rolled it down the face of the mountain a half-mile away across the big bowl of valley. It zoomed across valley floor, headed straight for me. A wall of white slammed against the mountain below my feet and exploded upward like an ocean wave. I could feel the temperature drop.

"Sounds good to me," I told Kim's voice. The bright white powder rolled over me like a benediction. "But call me back this evening," I yelled. "I'm kind of busy right now."

It was a powerful sign. Something beautiful was blowing in. Kim came. She stayed for the best part of that year. She was big-boned but beautiful, with a strong jaw and long straight hair and perfect American teeth. She was the best kind of hippie, sweet and sensitive, kind, but neat and tidy, even prim.

Kim was loopy, sentimental, hardworking, and utterly flexible. The animals loved her, and I think she loved them even more. She did chores without being told first. She made marvelous salads and left poems on the kitchen table. She had a valid drivers' license. Patrick's eyesight is bad, he gave up driving soon after we moved to Spain, and having another driver was a luxury. Kim didn't mind the car windows were smeared by dog noses. She often, on her own impulse, wiped away the smears. She stayed in the apple-green single bedroom upstairs, and was soon part of the family.

Patrick and I are idealists. We treat our helpers and casual laborers like co-workers. Pilgrims often worked for food or a little cash, back when we first arrived – some of them were skilled tradesmen, and good instructors. They taught me how to mix cement and meringues, how to make Thai chicken curry and tell a sprain from a broken bone.

Kim came to work, and stayed longer than any of them, and got a lot closer. She worked quietly, sometimes invisibly, and kept our house warm and clean – the house shines when she is there, so we call her "Shimmering Kim." Kim was tuned-in to the Camino magic. We expected coincidences when she was around. And animals. She has a real juju with critters.

I named the grey dog Lulu, after a tragic opera diva. The brindle, all elbows and angles, I called Knobby. Kim changed the spelling to "Nabi." Even though it sounded the same, "Nabi means 'butterfly' in Korean," Kim said. "And in Persian it's "prophet."

And so the foundling hounds caught a bit of shimmer.

3

KISS THE BABY

The men hauled themselves out of the rain and into the salon. Frenchmen. Brothers, they said. They were wet through and dirty, but their hiking equipment was of fine quality. They showered, and we hung their wet things on the clotheslines in the living room. In winter we resign ourselves to mud and puddles and laundry lines. The floors are terra-cotta tile, so the mess does no harm. It's just not pretty.

We only know a few words of French. The men didn't speak English, or Spanish. One of them, Martin, produced a wondrous computer translation device. Kim loves pilgrims, even French ones — Kim walked her first Camino across France.

It rains in January, and once in a while it snows. The temperature never drops far below freezing, but the wind is what gets you. The Meseta is a gently rolling plain, a bit like the bottom of the ocean. Come spring it's even more oceanic, when the barley and oats are high and the wind rolls over the surface in long waves.

Thousands of years ago the Meseta was a shallow ocean, a very high-altitude lake – Moratinos is almost 900 meters above sea level. That's higher than a lot of mountains, even though it looks flat. The real mountains, the Picos de Europa, start about 50 kilometers north of us. We see them when the sky is clear, tromping like Mastodons along the horizon east to west. They are not far, but they inhabit another weather system. We can see it snowing up there, even when it's clear down here. I love the mountains, but I wouldn't want to live there.

"It's going to snow," the pilgrim's machine told Kim. "Didier knows all about the weather. He can feel snow in his fingers and wrists."

We passed Martin's laptop computer around, so we all knew what was said. Patrick held up his gnarled hands to show them that he, too, felt the weather there sometimes. The older man, Didier, cackled.

"My brother Didier is a shepherd," Martin typed. "He works outdoors all days."

"A shepherd! That's a wonderful job, a useful job," Patrick exclaimed. "I wish I'd been a shepherd."

"What is your job, Martin?" Kim tapped into the translator.

"I am an investment banker," the answer came, "at a private bank in Toulouse."

From down the street came to sound of the church bell, the half-hour warning. Mass time.

"Come with us to church," Kim typed. "It's Three Kings Day. A big holiday. Pilgrims are welcome."

Epiphany, or Three Kings Day, is huge in Spain, the equal of Christmas in other places. Christmas is a religious holiday, when families go to church and feast together. But Three Kings — 12 days later — is when the gifts arrive. With New Year's Eve dropped into the mix, the holiday season in Spain goes on for weeks.

Three Kings Day is always cold and misty. The butane heaters were cranked up high in the little church, but bone-cracking cold rose from the stone foundations and chilled our ankles. Butane fumes make me wheeze, but Mass rarely lasts more than a half hour.

We took our places in our customary pews, muffled in layers. The opening chorus rolled forth with puffs of steam. We roared like dragons, each in our own key, praising God in the half light of the gray day. At the end of the service someone in the back clicked on a tinny tape of Christmas carols, and children's voices chanted a pop "Noel." The men stood up, and in order, youngest to oldest, they trooped to the front of the altar. Wee Don Santiago stood grinning in his too-big robes, cradling a doe-eyed plaster baby Jesus doll.

Each man in turn bent to kiss its tiny, bare knee. Padre Santiago wiped it with a handkerchief after each kiss, to cut down on germs. The women went next. And when they'd all done their deed, Padre Santiago turned to our pewful of foreigners and smiled. We had to, too.

Patrick, a hardened agnostic, went first. Then me, then Kim. The French brothers went last. When Didier's turn came, he fell to his knees before the priest, took the doll from his hands, and gave it a big, wet smacker right in its little face. He hugged it tenderly to his breast for a moment. Moratinos made a sharp inhale, and let it go when he handed back Baby Jesus and returned to his seat. The carol snapped off suddenly, but Didier smiled on for hours.

"My brother is very religious. He loves children. He loves dolls," Louis explained. "He is simple."

Back at home at dinnertime, Kim gave Didier a little teddy-bear keychain she'd kept clipped to her pack. We felt good, having pilgrims there for Epiphany. Holidays can be tough, at least for me – my children and mom and sisters are thousands of miles away. That year just one gift was given, to someone who was almost a child.

The brothers left the next morning, fed and watered, wined and dined, showered and shaved. They left nothing in the donation box.

"An investment banker! Really?" I said. "He has to know better."

"Camino amnesia," Kim said.

"Pricks," Patrick said.

4

ZARAGOZA CHOOKS

Two Australian girls came through, university students hiking through their summer break – February is summer down there. They knew about chickens (they called them "chooks") so we put them to work cleaning up the chicken house. They stretched out the job for three days.

Three days of warm floors, good beds, and hot food, a home where English was spoken. One was a radical lesbian performance artist. The other was a classics scholar. She talked into the night with Patrick about Plato, Aristotle, and Aristophanes, what makes an action wrong or a joke funny.

We have a shower, and plenty more food than we need, and three pilgrim beds in the salon. We don't have room for more than five pilgrims at a time. We keep the numbers low, so we can look them each in the eye, learn their names, hear their story if they want to tell it.

I come from a long line of that — my dad sometimes brought home hung-over soldiers and sailors from the Enlisted Men's club and let them sleep it off on the living room couch. My grandfather brought bums from the bus station and sat them down to dinner alongside the family. His father Claude helped to found Vandergrift, a steel town in western Pennsylvania. Claude France was a big man in town, but the grave next to his in the cemetery is occupied by Albert, a half-blind hobo Claude found bumming around the depot one morning. Claude took the man home and gave him work. When Albert died 14 years later, they laid him to rest with the family.

We have precedent. And in Moratinos, we have room. So far, none of our "guests" has robbed or assaulted us, even though a few of them were scary. Some are not pilgrims. They are migrant workers, tramps, or even fugitives. Just about everyone arrives exhausted. They don't have the energy to misbehave.

Patrick and I walk the dogs each morning, and that's when we plan out the day or the week ahead. We tell one another which David Bowie song is stuck in our head, and decide what's to eat that day and who's preparing it. Out in the fields we often let the dogs run loose. Moratinos stands in a great ocean of fields, home to millions of mice and moles. Una and Tim were obsessive mousers, and they'd dig halfway to China to catch and kill a single scrawny rodent. They soon showed Nabi and Lulu their technique.

The dogs ran two miles to our one, chasing one another,

snarling and snapping. The greyhounds showed us the splendor of their breed, the spectacle of two hounds together going flat-out over open ground. Trouble was, the galgos still didn't know their names. They didn't come when we called to them. Catching them was a challenge.

One Sunday after Mass Pablo asked me to stop by their house on the way home. This was not unusual. I often had a coffee and a visit after church. Their family was a favorite of mine.

But this Sunday, instead of the coffee pot, there was a chicken on the kitchen counter, plucked and drawn and ready for the pot. "Have a look," Pablo said.

On its breast and neck were tears, punctures. Bite marks. Nabi had evidently taken a detour during that morning's walk. She'd slipped into Pablo's yard, grabbed a red hen, and snapped her neck. Pablo saw it happen.

"And look at this!" Maribel said, pulling up a saucepan. Inside was a whirl of guts. She pushed aside a flap, and there were three little eggs-in-progress in the chute. It looked almost comical, but this wasn't funny. Pablo and Maribel had been more than kind to us since we'd arrived, but they looked very blank-faced now.

"Hija, you cannot let those galgos run loose in the town," Pablo said. I felt myself turn red. I felt like I'd butchered the hen myself, with my own teeth.

"Yes," I said, struggling to find words. "My apologies. I will in the future keep the galgos attached. The chicken will be... renewed. Refunded." Future tense, conditional? My Spanish was not equal to this. "Is Angela at home this weekend?" I asked.

"I am here, Rebekah," came a grave voice from the doorway, in English. Angela was still in her flannel pajamas. "The galgo killed the chicken," she said.

"Yes. And I am very sorry," I said. "I will replace the chicken," I said. "Please tell your mom and dad I will replace the chicken. I have six new hens. But they are not red hens. I hope that's alright. A good laying hen from Zaragoza."

"I will tell them," Angela said, brushing sleep from her eyes. "I will get dressed. I will come and have a visit."

I slipped out the door, abashed. This was serious. But we had Angela, thank God.

Angela was 30 years old, the youngest person in Moratinos. She was an elementary school teacher who specialized in English. She and I bonded right away when we moved in. She enjoyed having native English speakers to chat with, and we very much needed her help as we navigated the strange, deep waters of rural Castilla y Leon.

I went straight to our henhouse, grabbed up a new pullet, and popped her into a plastic shopping bag. (Shopping bags have a hypnotic effect on chickens.) I carried it over to Maribel's place and handed it over. "I've had her only a month, and she's laying already," I said.

Maribel peered inside the bag. The hen peered up at her. "The chicken is black," she said.

"She lays a big brown egg every day," I told her. "She is young. She is a nice girl."

"Give her a chance," Angela said. "It's a hen from Zaragoza. Zaragoza is in Spain. It's a Spanish chicken, mom!"

Maribel shrugged her shoulders. "Vamos a ver," she said. "We'll see."

We'd kept hens from the start. There was a chicken coop out back when we moved in, and we put up a fence and made a home for hens almost as soon we made a cozy nest for ourselves. Somehow, however, young hens for sale at the feed-store were always reddish-brown. We made pets of them at first. Blodwyn, the leader of the pack, was particularly bright and affectionate, fond of sitting in our laps and cooing softly in the background whenever I spoke on the telephone. After that first generation of hens died off, I returned to what we call "the Chicken Boutique," a looming old warehouse by the Sahagún stoplight with the word "HENS" painted in faded letters on the outside wall. I stepped into the cackling gloom, and once my eyes adjusted I found the proprietress nestled into a busted easy chair among stacks of feed-bags and celebrity magazines. Cages along the wall fluttered with life.

"Speak," said the voice from the chair.

"I would like to buy some hens," I said. "Point-of-lay pullets." (I'd looked up the word first.)

"How many?" the voice said.

"Six," I said. "But I wonder if you have other kinds of chickens."

"What kind of chickens do you mean?" the chicken lady asked, heaving herself up from her chair.

I had never seen her out of her chair. She looked a lot like her merchandise. She looked at me sideways, brushing straw and dust from her clothes. Wattles waggled under her chin.

"I mean laying hens," I told her. "But another variety. Black hens, for instance. Or white. Or speckled. I've seen them other places in Spain."

"Yes. There are black hens," the lady said. "They are from Zaragoza." She enunciated the word carefully and loudly. (Foreigners will understand you if you shout at them very slowly.)

"Za-ra-go-za," echoed off the rafters and feedbags and cages.

"Zaragoza," I said, lisping it like a Castilian. "Yes. And I saw some speckled ones up in Asturias. That's even closer."

"I can get the ones from Zaragoza," the lady said. "Next week. You have to order six. And they'll cost you."

"How much?" I asked. I braced myself.

"Six Euros. Six. Six Euros each. Point of lay. Six times six. Up front."

"I have twelve Euros in my hand. One-third down. Live animals," I told her. (I learned about ordering young animals by watching the Amish at the livestock auction in Belknap, Pennsylvania. Amish farmers would fit right into Castile.)

I lay the money down on the counter, a ten and a two-euro coin. "Si, señora." I said. "Let's do this. A third up front. Live animals."

She looked at me from under her side-swept bangs. "For dead animals, you must go to the butcher," she said. I laughed, but she didn't. We recognized something in one another. She scrawled something on a bit of paper and handed it to me. Chicken scratch.

"Let me ask you a question," she said.

"Vale," I countered in my most fluent Castellano.

"Our hens. The ones we sell here. The brown ones. Castilian hens."

"Yeah," I said. "Castilian reds."

She inhaled, filled her breast.

"What's wrong with Castilian hens?"

Zaragoza came through for me. Maribel's black hen delivered at least one brown egg each day for the rest of her life. She justified my gamble at the Chicken Boutique, atoned for my killer galgo and my ignorance, and proved to people all over town that black hens can, indeed, deliver. The Chicken Boutique now keeps them in stock, along with little white hens from Oviedo.

5

BORN IN THIS ROOM

In the afternoon a knock came on the gate. Outside stood a lady with big hair, and a swarthy little man. The man pinched a cigarette in his thumb and forefinger and squinted into his private cloud of smoke.

"I beg your pardon. I am Rogelia," the lady said, "I was just visiting over at Pilar's house, and she said you wouldn't mind if I came over. I grew up in this house. I am only in town for a few moments," she said, looking round nervously. "Do you think I could see inside, just into the patio? I won't take much of your time."

"Of course! You are welcome!" I said. I waved them inside. The man threw down his cigarette and blew the last smoke out his nostrils. "I am her husband," he said. "We heard that Conchi had sold the place."

"I haven't been here since my brother died," Rogelia said. "Not since, what? 1976? And even then, not inside. I know Conchi would have improved it."

"We've changed a lot of things, too," I said, stepping into the patio with them. "We bought it in 2006."

Rogelia stepped into the patio. The farmyard she'd known was paved in patchwork cement, the walls whitewash streaked with rust and mud, with a sheep trough and fruit trees, block-and-tackles and buckets. Most of that was gone, replaced with a little lawn, an arch of ivy, an herb garden. The layout was the same, but we'd gutted and rebuilt the house, reroofed, wired, plumbed, tiled and paved and painted it all. All but the barn. They stood, turning, looking. The sun beat down.

Inside were electric lights, a kitchen, high ceilings, canary song. Upstairs, in Kim's apple-green bedroom, Rogelia started to cry.

"You still have my parents' bed," she said. "I was born in this room."

In what's now the upstairs bath, her father had dried rushes and canes. He made baskets, she said, caned chairs, wove rugs out of plants that grew along the creeks and springs. We'd found a few of those things in the barn when we moved in. Patrick went and got a small, dusty basket that stood a bit awry.

"Is this one of his works?" he asked.

"It could be," Rogelia said.

"Please, take this with you if you like," Patrick said. "A remembrance."

"No, thank you," she said. "Our apartment is small and modern. We have no need of rustic things."

The upstairs hall seemed to catch and hold her still. She looked for a long time out the front windows, over the patio and the roofs of the town, the church, the fields south. I didn't tell her I'd seen a ghost there, standing at that same window. I think it was her brother.

Rogelia's brother Mario was the last person to live in our house. He was left alone after his mother died, and he could not cope with the solitude. One morning Edu went to weed his garden and found Mario's shoes and socks and his neatly-folded jacket by the edge of the well. Mario's body was at the bottom.

"The town is almost the same from up here," Rogelia said. "But the house? It is so different. So pretty now. Smaller than I remembered.

"You were a little girl when you left?"

"I left when I was young," Rogelia said. "I didn't come back."

"Oh my," I said. "I hope this doesn't stir up sad memories."

"Oh, no. Life is so much better in the city," she said. "We don't have the wind blowing through the house all winter."

She surveyed the front patio again, and the granary that's now the kitchen. "The place is much cleaner without the sheep and mules," she said. "But you should've kept the ceilings. This house catches the wind, you know. You should've kept the windows small. It holds in the warmth. When it is low, it's cozy."

And dark, I thought to myself. When we moved in, the ceilings upstairs were so low we bashed our foreheads on the doorways. We had to raise the ceilings, so we eliminated them altogether. The ceilings soar now into warm wood, at roof-level. It's drafty, but it's bright.

Rogelia said she was glad she'd seen the house again, but sad, too. She asked us not to tell her sister she had been there. I told her she is always welcome to visit.

"Thank you," she said, matter-of-factly. "You are kind. But I will not see this place again."

6

FROM WHERE DID YOU FLY?

About 5 p.m. the telephone rang – eight pilgrims at Terradillos, the village 3 kilometers before ours. They'd hiked all the way from Carrion de los Condes, a good 27 kilometers, to find the pilgrim albergue there was closed.

We told them to come on over. We'd sort things out when they arrived.

Eight pilgrims is too many. We had five pilgrim beds, and one of them already had Kim in it. The throng rolled in just after sundown, footsore and cranky. Four of them accepted my offer of a ride into Sahagun, where the big pilgrim shelter was open for business. The remainder – two Koreans and two Germans – stayed with us. We bumped-up the dinner with another jar of lentils and another loaf of bread. Everyone was tucked into bed by 10 p.m.

So many pilgrims in February! We were used to one or two per week, but this was odd. Winter pilgrims are usually solitary creatures, but that winter the pilgrims came in twos and threes, and now in even larger bunches.

That year, 2010, was a Holy Year. The feast day of St. James the Apostle fell on Sunday, so pilgrims who walked the walk, confessed their sins, prayed and worshiped at his shrine at Santiago de Compostela qualified for a special Holy Year indulgence – a full remission of all their venial sins. For a faithful Catholic, that's a hard deal to pass up. And even unbelievers, evidently, were excited to get that grace in a small window of sacred time. We'd been warned to expect waves of pilgrims that year, but we never expected to see so many in the dead of winter.

Moratinos is not a natural stopping-place. It falls before or behind the ten to twenty miles most people can walk in a day. Pilgrims came to our house usually because they were up against it: because the albergues to the east – simple pilgrim shelters – closed their doors at the owners' whims in winter. When that happened, we got them half-frozen, wet through, and worn-out.

Pilgrims are people in motion. They come, they eat, they sleep, and they move on. Their needs are basic, their time with us is short. Ninety percent of them are remarkably low-maintenance, considering the demands they make on their bodies.

Moratinos is half-way along the usual trail from the French frontier. By the time they get to us, the pilgrims have already walked 210 miles. They are fit, lean, in the groove, but they sleep in close quarters. They pass germs among themselves.

Sometimes they share them with us. That year, Patrick caught bronchitis. Kim and I had nasty colds. I passed mine to Angela, who passed it on to her students.

We had other troubles. Murphy the cat flipped the laptop computer onto the floor, and the damage could not be repaired. The water heater started switching itself off in the night. Kim made us a bigger, brighter donation box, because the old one somehow escaped pilgrims' notice. We were spending more money on pilgrims than we were taking in.

The water heater stopped working altogether, and the repairman waited a week to arrive. I had a single shower that week, over at Angela's house. It was embarrassing to ask, and I think Maribel and Pablo were a bit embarrassed to have me over there, doing something naked in their downstairs bathroom.

If worse came to worst, we could've checked into a hotel in Sahagun, only six miles away. But once again, despite their second thoughts, the neighbors came through for us. Our neighbors were kind to us, right from the start. Our neighbors are why we chose to settle in tiny Moratinos.

Only 18 people lived in town. About 14 of them stayed through the winter. Our decision to live in Moratinos all year, every year, is a fact of continued fascination for people throughout the region.

"Even in winter? In such a little town? How could you?" ask the barber, mechanic, accountant, pilgrim.

"We sold our house in America. We don't have another home to go to," we tell them. "And we love the *tranquilidad.*"

"You'll get plenty of that!" they say, laughing, rolling their eyes, gnashing their teeth. "I couldn't stand it. And you left England for that? You left America!"

"This is home now," we say, primly. "We're Palentinos, *de pura cepa.* Purebreds." That always gets a laugh. One of my proudest moments came at the funeral of a neighbor in San Nicolas, the next village. Resti died, co-owner of the only restaurant-pub within 4 kilometers. The short walk from the church to the cemetery was too much for one tiny old lady, so I offered her my elbow. She clung on like a limpet, and after the service she asked if I was "one of the Moratinos *foresteros*" a visitor, a bird of passage.

"Rebekah is not a forestero," snapped Remedios. "She is a *vecina.* An *amiga.*" A neighbor. A friend. Castellanos don't use those worlds lightly. I thought I might cry.

For a long time we were unique, almost exotic. When the post office received mail for an odd, foreign-looking addressee, they brought to our house. A newspaper reporter interviewed us, and spelled our names wrong. I started training English-speaking volunteers to be hospitaleros, hosts in the

Spanish network of non-profit pilgrim shelters. I became an informal liaison for the Spanish camino federation with camino associations in the US, Canada, South Africa, and Australia. When an English-speaking pilgrim got into trouble, the albergue owner, police, or medical service called us in to help out. It was a little flattering, and a little much, too.

It didn't last. More pilgrims took to the trail, and demand increased for beds and meals all along the track. Strangers came to town, search committees from non-profit pilgrim groups, entrepreneurs sniffing out opportunities. There was no pilgrim albergue in Moratinos, but it was only a matter of time. In late February, Bruno called.

Bruno was part of a pilgrim fraternity in Brescia, in Italy's industrial north. They wanted to start an albergue, and Bruno had come to town the summer before, scouting out likely sites. I'd showed him around town, introduced him to people, tracked down the owners of empty houses.

They'd bought the big old house on Calle Ontanon, Bruno said. A crew would arrive at the end of the month to transform it into the newest, best, most charitable albergue on the Camino. They'd need a place to stay, at least until the weather broke. Two or three of them. Two or three months, then they could move into the new place.

Could they stay with us? There was no other place in town.

Patrick said yes. He usually does. He shouldn't have.

Nabi and Lulu filled out. Their hair was short and thin, and we wondered if they shivered from cold or nerves. We put jackets on them, but they tore them off. The pair slept together in the deep hay in the barn. They walked beautifully on the lead, but shied away and hid behind us when strangers approached.

They were lanky, they walked on their tippy-toes like Barbie dolls. Una Dog bossed them around. Una bossed everyone. We let her do what she liked. We knew her days were numbered, so we spoiled her.

Una had been with us since the start of our partnership. In one week's time in the summer of 2003, Patrick and I married one another on a riverbank in Maumee, Ohio. Patrick retired from his newsroom boss job at the Toledo newspaper, and I resigned my reporter position. We moved to a busted old steel-and-glass town outside Pittsburgh, where I started a new job at the big metropolitan paper.

We rented a rickety house on a rural road. Una showed up a day later. It was love at first sight, Patrick and Una — Patrick's always had a thing for difficult, scruffy, intelligent girls. Una helped Patrick ease into retirement. She kept him active, kept him engaged through a time he may otherwise have withdrawn. She was stubborn, infuriating and funny. Three years later, when the time came to move to Spain, Una came in a crate on the long, red-eye flight from Pittsburgh to Atlanta to Madrid. Patrick met us at the airport.

I was carrying excess baggage, struggling to get my things off the luggage belt and onto a cart before reporting to the Oversize Bags desk, where I expected to find the dog. A Spanish sailor stepped in to help me. Then Una's crate came shivering down the chute and onto the belt with the regular luggage, the dog inside baying like a banshee. She'd come through just fine. The man helped me wrestle the crate off the belt. He smiled wide as Una and I reunited.

"From where did you fly?" he asked me in careful English.

"We came on the Atlanta flight," I told him. The man looked through the wire door at the grinning, stinking mutt inside.

"You brought *that* from America?" he asked.

I'd left behind a fine career and a pretty home, my mom and sisters, my two grown children and a fat pet ferret named Sid Vicious. But to leave Una behind would've been unthinkable.

The Meseta is dog heaven. The hills are alive with rodents, and Una was a terrier, born to seek them out and kill them. Other dogs blew in, and Una tolerated each one, once she made clear the rules. All food and toys were subject to seizure. No animal was stroked without her being cuddled just as well.

Una walked thousands of miles with us over our years together – or she ran while we walked. She was a dirty dog, a cur, sometimes maddeningly disobedient. Patrick and I were too old and spoiled to have any more children, so we had Una. Or maybe Una had us.

In 2009 we learned that a persistent limp in Una's rear right leg was bone cancer. The veterinarian amputated the leg, but the disease had moved to her lungs. Still, for more than a year Una soldiered on with three legs. When we set loose the greyhounds for one of their spectacular chases, Una bounced through the fields behind them, yapping and snapping – at least for a little while.

Late winter sent us far afield, the back of the car loaded with dogs, to walk trails we'd noticed back when the sky was blue and fields were green. We skipped church one sunny Sunday morning to walk along a ridge above Ledigos. That was the Camino de Santiago, back before it was re-routed to benefit more villages. We parked near the blacktop and walked eastward up a rutted tractor path. The dogs ran free in fallow fields that fell away on either side. Up and up we went past battered Camino waymarks. The clouds grew grey and heavy until they turned to mist around us. Far away down the valley, the Rio Cueza roared and foamed, a grey ribbon threaded through the brown burlap fields.

It's lonely country, wind-whipped. The meseta is "the granary of Spain," but the ground in our neighborhood is heavy clay, not very fertile. I'd tried gardening in our back yard with little success. I eyed a massive mountain of cow manure looming along the path, waiting in the rain for the farmer to plow it into the field. I wondered if he'd miss any, if I took a little for my vegetable beds.

Walking in the cold rain, I envisioned green beans and tomato plants, green leaves in sunshine, the garden of the months to come.

Patrick and I were off to London for a few days. Kim would watch the dogs and keep house. Our friends David and Malin would come and stay and work while we were gone. They would build five raised-bed garden frames to enclose my raggedy vegetable patches. I would need to fill up the frames eventually with soil and dung. I wondered who I could ask, where I could get fertilizer. It wasn't as easy as it looked.

I smiled at myself. I wanted people to give me shit.

7

POPULAR HERMITS

I like to imagine Patrick and I are hermits, living a solitary, contemplative existence in a lonesome place. Reality says different. People keep coming to our house, and we keep letting them in. I understand a lot of historic hermits had that problem. Just call yourself a hermit, and people will find you irresistible.

It doesn't help much that I involve myself in causes, and organizations, and projects.

Organizations are important and useful, but I do not work very well with governing boards. When I see a problem, I do something to solve it. I don't ask permission first. I don't wait for the next board meeting. I am a loose cannon.

Many people seem to like me telling them what to do. Organizations continue putting me in charge of things. Sometimes it works.

The first hospitalero trainee showed up on Friday night: Richard, an English vicar in a camper van. He could sleep out there, he said, although I could tell he didn't really want to. It was windy, and in February the cold pushes its way through every crack. What was I going to do, put him on the street? We had an extra bed, at least for that night. I put him in there.

Back before we moved to Spain, Patrick and I became volunteer hospitaleros – hosts at non-profit, bare-bones pilgrim shelters along the way to Santiago. It was an odd way to spend our holidays, but a good way to meet interesting, if exhausted, people from all over the world. It's a great way to get to know Spain, and Spanish, and Spaniards. We did a lot of volunteering at a variety of places.

Once we got our own place on the Camino, I put my experience to work once or twice each year, helping to train new albergue volunteers. It was the only English-language training program in Spain, and it proved nominally popular for a while. In 2009, I adapted the program into an online, interactive curriculum, so faraway fraternities in Australia, South Africa, and New Zealand and Eastern Europe could use "distance learning" to train their willing workers. At the last minute, the Spanish federation board axed it.

"You have to look at them, shake their hands, hear their voices," said Anai, the lady in charge. "We're forming a brotherhood here. You have to hug these people, you have to give them some time, some love. You can't do that on the internet."

I was peeved, but I saw her point. There really is a brotherhood feeling among hospitaleros, and if things get out of hand at your albergue, you can always call for help from the next hospitalero along the way. One-on-one training is also a good way to weed out people whose reasons for volunteering are less-than noble, or who just aren't well enough to do the job.

I didn't toss away all my hard work. I boiled it down, shifted it into written form, and sent it wholesale to confraternities and pilgrim associations in the Americas, the Antipodes and Africa. And there it lives on, taught to this day in modified forms, under many peoples' names, to dozens of willing workers.

Like the bumper-stickers say, if you love something, set it free.

I kept training people "live," a few at a time, but I did not spend entire weekends with them, stewing lentils and counting out donations and endowing them with initiatory scarves and scallop shells. I trained my hospitaleros in a single long day. I gave them the basics. I knew that once they showed up at their volunteer post, they'd learn a whole lot more by just doing the job.

Two more trainees arrived on foot Saturday morning: a fastidious Dane and a roly-poly Dutchman. We started early with the training, we sat and chatted and I lectured them through the bits about what is the Spanish Federation of Amigos de Santiago, what are "albergues," and why it's important to keep some places on the pilgrim trail on a donation-only basis. I was launching into the part about being absolutely flexible when the doorbell rang.

The Italians were here, with suitcases. They spoke no English. They were two days early.

They were three men laden with tools and great expectations. They were starting work tomorrow on the new albergue down the street, but right now they wanted some lunch, they said. Did we have anything ready? Was there any food in the house?

How many ways can I say 'no?' I wondered. No food here. No restaurant either.

"Go to Sahagun and eat. I'm training these people right now. We'll come up with some dinner if you'll pick up some vegetables in town," I told them. I spoke to them in Spanish, which they seemed to understand.

Someone would have to sleep someplace else. We were going to have to be absolutely flexible.

"Richard," I said to the Englishman, "can you sleep in your camper tonight?"

Richard didn't understand me, because I was still

speaking Spanish. I said it again in English. Richard was cool with that, he said. The Italians wandered into the salon.

"This room is too small for three people," one of them said. (Italian is very close to Spanish. I do not speak Italian, but I understand it well enough.)

I excused myself from the trainees, and went to ask Patrick to tell the Italian guys to get a room in Sahagun. Patrick was out back chopping firewood. The unhappy Italian tapped me on the shoulder with his finger. He tapped hard.

"Where is the closet? Where can I hang my coat?" he asked. "This place is small."

"This place isn't a hotel. It's a stop for pilgrims," I told him. "Pilgrims don't need closets. You're not going to find anything better for five Euros, my friend."

He looked hurt. Too many people at once. I was being too brusque. I slipped my hand into my pocket and felt the calming little Rosary there.

"You are here two days early," I told the man. "These people were here first. We don't have room tonight. No food now. Go to Sahagun," I said. "Have dinner here with us. Bring back some wine, some bread, and some lettuce." I felt like the chicken lady, enunciating for the foreigner.

He shrugged.

I didn't think he understood me. Bruno reappeared, told me "OK, OK!" and they rumbled back out the gate.

I sat back down at the table, shifted back into teacher mode. "You want to run a pilgrim albergue, it's not all guitars and sing-songs and sangria sunsets," I said. "You have to sop up a lot of filth, lance a lot of blisters, hug people who smell bad. You must always be ready to say "I don't know." Or just "No." You have to cook lots of lentils and beans. You need a really strong, well-developed inner life – a spirituality. Running an albergue is not a job for the hopeless, or the helpless."

The trainees' eyes glazed over. They already knew everything they needed to know. Hospitalero-ing isn't brain surgery, just about anybody with common sense can handle the usual two-week gig. But then came the next question. The Big One.

"Let's talk about running our own albergue," Richard said. "Everybody who walks the Camino thinks about buying a place and fixing it up and running his own albergue. Tell us about this place. Tell us about your dream!"

He was right. Almost every pilgrim spots an abandoned house along the Road somewhere and wonders: Why don't I throw over my "real life" and start again on the Camino?

I can hang out forever with jolly pilgrims, live low to the ground, become a part of the scene!

It happened to me, so I know. I discovered the Camino before most Americans did – I came to Spain in 1993 as a freelance travel journalist, a guest of the Tourist Office of Spain. We zipped along the Camino in a luxury van, slept in fancy hotels, walked only the most scenic bits of trail. Travel writing was a hustle back in those days. Spain gave us a star-spangled tour. In exchange, we joy-riding journos wrote glowing reports in North American magazines and newspapers about this "Camino de Santiago," an adventure tour-religious pilgrimage product they hoped would give northern Spain a tourism boost.

I did not disappoint. I sold Santiago stories to papers from Toronto to Miami. I started reading up on Spain, I learned a little Spanish. I took more trips to Spain, wrote about different parts of the country and its culture and cuisine, but the Camino kept calling my name. Finally, in 2001, I carved out six weeks of holiday time and walked the entire thing.

I fell in love. A couple of years later I trained in Toronto to be a hospitalera. I met powerful people there, founders, scholars, linguists, historians, preachers and teachers. They served the Camino from where they lived in the United States, Canada, Brazil, and the Netherlands. They flew to Spain periodically to walk and serve and study, and then they went back home to 'real life.' Between holidays, they dreamed Camino dreams.

Some of those people became my best friends, the companions of my second life.

I am a radical, and lucky for me my partner is equally open to radical ideas. Patrick and I took a long look at our comfortable American lives. Suburbia was not what we wanted any more. Something was calling us away.

So, after some years of planning, investing, and dreaming, we went. We sold everything, packed up what remained, and moved to our tiny Castilian pueblo. There followed another couple of years of anxiety, ignorance, sweat, and divine providence. It came together. The dream came true. We called the house "Peaceable Kingdom," even though Patrick thinks naming houses is pretentious.

Five years on, our lives looked idyllic to the casual observer. We had retirement income enough to support ourselves, so we didn't rely on pilgrim donations to keep us afloat. Our health was good, and we were happy with the care provided by the national medical system. We had our critters, and a nice house, and lots of nice pilgrims coming and going. Still, we knew that daily life in Moratinos would not suit most people – even people with long experience running hotels or non-profits.

Living and working with pilgrims on the Camino de Santiago is not a hobby. It's not a job. It is a calling. The Camino de Santiago is a sacred place, a holy road. People who come here to stay must be willing to be made holy as well.

It's that demanding, that rewarding. It is that costly, and harrowing, and transformative.

And it's hard as hell. They speak another language here. Regulations change, people fall in love, move away, die, burn out, fall out and go broke. Winters are long and boring, summers are hot and hectic. Spain is chaotic and corrupt, burdened with a bureaucracy that punishes small businesses and innovators. Almost every non-Spaniard I know who's tried to make a life on the Camino does not stay longer than five years or so.

It's sad, but true.

The Italians were gone to Sahagun, so the trainees made a huge pan of lasagna, and sat back down to learn some more while it baked. We hiked out to the holy well at San Martin de la Fuente, anointed one another's eyes with the healing spring water, and learned about making simple rituals.

When we returned we found a note in the mailbox. It said:

"Thanks for what you do for the pilgrims. Sorry we missed you."

No signature. Thirty Euros were folded inside.

It was all the money we made that day, but it was enough to pay everybody's way.

8

RETURN OF THE FUGITIVE

David is Dutch. Malin is Swedish. They met on the trail and fell in love with Spain, the Camino, and one another. They were 30-something professionals back at home, but each left a career and fiancée to live together along the trail. They were lovey-dovey, helpful and useful. They were the first people I taught to be hospitaleros.

David was a TV engineer back in Rotterdam. At our house he devised clever solutions when things mechanical or electronic failed. Malin was a vegetarian cook, a folk singer, a yoga teacher, daughter of a famous Swedish musician. She and David had become buskers. Their marionette danced and played the fiddle at festivals and street fairs. They lived in a Volkswagen camper van named Rusty. Rusty needed an overhaul.

Patrick and I were off to London for a few days.

Malin and David had been living for months in the snowy mountains above Astorga, and were ready for a break. Our house was warm and roomy. David could use the old donkey barn out back for a dry workspace – the van just barely fit inside. Malin and Kim would do some of the dustier cleaning jobs, the things I am most allergic-to.

We had more help than we really required, with Kim already there – but everyone knew and liked one another. There was plenty of food in the freezer and firewood in the shed. The Italians, now dubbed "the Mario Brothers," had gone back to Italy for a week or two. Everything seemed to be working out just fine.

David drove us in our car to the airport. He had Rusty all set up in the barn, he said, and Ryan would arrive that evening to help with the bodywork. Ryan had decided to come while we were gone, when he wouldn't be in our way, David said.

"Ryan. You don't mean Ryan from Pittsburgh, do you?"

"Yeah. He helped you guys out with a roof last summer, didn't he?"

Patrick said something unprintable. "I didn't know you knew Ryan, David."

"Ryan is a welder. A professional metal worker," David said. "I need someone like him. The frame needs some welding, and I am not a good welder, myself."

"We told Ryan to stay out of Moratinos!" I said, trying to keep the anger out of my voice. "Nobody told us he was coming back."

"To stay at our house," Paddy said. "This isn't good news, David."

"My Gott," David said. "I didn't know it was so bad. Ryan said there was some trouble about a girl, but I did not ask for details. For me, it is 'don't ask, don't tell.'"

"He wasn't supposed to ever come back," I said.

The road rolled on by under our wheels. Paddy and I exchanged glances.

"David, keep him away from Pablo. And Angela. And keep him out of the bodega. The guy drinks, and then he gets stupid."

"He starts to *sing,*" Patrick said.

"I am not happy about this," I added.

"I am very sorry," David said. "I didn't know. I'll keep an eye on him."

"I'll email Angela, tell her not to come home this weekend, unless she wants to see Ryan. I doubt she will."

"Holy cow," Patrick said. "And here we are, off to bleeding London."

Ryan had come to us the previous summer from Hungary. I met him online, during a big, exciting season of Pittsburgh Steelers football. He was a friendly guy, skilled, looking for work anywhere in Europe. We needed a builder, and what's not to like about a union sheet-metal worker from the old hometown? He came on the bus, walked in with an enormous Army-issue pack, stinking from the road and smiling wide behind a cigarette.

He was hardworking, funny, and willing to learn. He'd never heard of the Camino, but he got on well with the pilgrims. He went straight to work replacing the barn roof. He was scenic up there, shirtless and trim, singing along to Leonard Cohen hits, slinging tiles.

Ryan had a big baritone voice. He knew many songs, but he had no volume control. Every tune, be it Broadway, ballad or lullaby, was delivered full-blast, from the bottom of his heart.

Angela came over that afternoon. We sat on the patio, shelled peas, and spoke in English. She showed me a drawing done by a talented student, and enthused about her classroom in the new school buildings in Salas.

After years of cramming and taking exams, Angela had finally become a grammar-school English teacher. She worked in a remote town in Burgos province, and was back home now for the summer break. She spent a lot of time at our house, enjoying the ever-changing cast of characters. She was a gentle soul, young for her age, a tiny slip of a woman – it was hard not to think of her as a girl. Patrick called her "Little Angela," and she didn't mind.

She saw the suntanned man on the roof. Angela often sparked and sparkled at our handsome international guests, especially the musical ones.

While he labored in the sun, I told her how Ryan found us, how Pittsburgh natives often help each other out even when they're far from home, even if they've never met. Ryan finally clambered down and introduced himself.

That evening, out for a walk with Una and Tim, I saw Ryan and Angela near the Rio de los Templarios. They were holding hands. "That didn't take long," I thought.

Ryan stayed up late that night drinking new wine, telling us about his hitch in the Marines, his work in the mills and metal shops on Neville Island and McKeesport and Blawnox – home places to me. He hadn't been back for years, he said – he'd let his passport expire, and didn't have money enough to pay his way out of that bureaucratic mess. He picked up languages easily, did auto-body work, drifted job to job across Europe, singing and playing guitar on the streets when he couldn't find work building or fixing things. It wasn't a bad life, but he missed his Mom. And he'd really like to settle down sometime soon, he said. Find a nice girl.

A girl like Angela.

"How can you settle down without any ID? How can you get a proper job?" I asked him. "What do you have to offer a nice girl?"

"If I got married I would be legal automatically," he said, "especially once we had a baby. I can work just about anywhere."

"You've thought about this before, I see."

"I've been in love before," he said. "I fall really, really hard."

"This is a slow, slow place, Ryan. People are conservative here. Take your time."

He just looked at me from under his lush eyelashes.

"Easy for you to say," he said.

And so Ryan and Angela fell madly in love.

For ten days Ryan worked like a devil all day, then cleaned up and went out for walks with Angela in the evening. He met Pablo and Maribel, her parents. He took Angela to dinner at La Barrunta, the restaurant in the next town. Angela took him in her car up to Saldaña, to the big Thursday market. She seemed to glory in all the attention he paid her, the long poems, the love songs sung for the whole world to hear.

One morning I walked the dogs down the road alongside Pablo's perfect vegetable garden, and there was Angela with a sickle, cutting the alfalfa that sprouted wild along the path. It´s free, she said, and the rabbits love it. It brings in the mother rabbits' milk.

Angela left the sickle and wheelbarrow and walked up the trail with me. I asked her where she'd been, told her I missed seeing her around the place.

"Ryan's there in the day, working," she said. "The evenings are intense enough, the day I rather enjoy having to myself."

"Oh?" I asked. "Is there trouble? I thought you guys were crazy about one another."

"I don't want to hold his hand all the time," she said, a little exasperated. "I know he's been lonely a long time, but he always has to be touching me. Over in Sahagún yesterday we met some of my friends from school, I hadn't seen them for months. But Ryan didn't want to go have a drink. He didn't want me to go with them. He just stood there with his arm around me, like he couldn't wait for them to go away."

"Jesus," I said. "That's creepy."

"Is this how Americans are?" she asked. "I don't want to be culturally insensitive. I don't want to offend him. I don't know how to tell him... I'd hate to hurt his feelings."

"It's not an American thing," I said. "It's machismo. He's mistaking love for ownership."

"Please," she said, "can you tell him to slow down? I don't want him to go away. I just want him to back off a little. We only just met."

So at lunchtime I told Ryan to back off. Patrick did, too.

He just cocked that eyebrow at us. "She's a girl. She's playing hard to get," he said with a grin.

"She's not playing, Ryan. Respect her," I said, annoyed.

Patrick looked him in the eye. "You hurt that girl, I'll kick your ass."

"I understand why you feel like that," Ryan said. "She makes me feel really protective, too. I'd die before I'd ever hurt Angela."

That night Ryan and Angela went out to Sahagun's only discotheque. They danced and dined with Angela's friends, and posted smiling photos to their Facebook accounts.

Our house was quiet. I often stay up late, and about midnight I got out our guest register to make sure that night's pilgrim had signed-in.

I noticed Ryan's signature on the previous page. His name was Ryan Svoboda, from Pittsburgh, Pennsylvania. But he'd signed himself in as Ron Simmons, from Youngstown, Ohio.

I was a newspaper reporter for 22 years. I felt a familiar prickle: A lie. Was he careless, or did he think we wouldn't notice? Or maybe he wanted us to.

I sat down at the computer and checked out his ID. It didn't take long. Ryan was wanted by the U.S. marshals. Four years earlier he had jumped bail and fled, charged in two states with sexual assault, battery, taking a minor across state lines, possession of firearms. There was no mistaking the face in the mugshots. There was Ryan, on the sexual predators list.

He was out there in the dark, with little Angela.

I woke up Patrick. I showed him the website.

"My God, what do we do?" he said. We made tea. We talked. Should we call the police? No, we shouldn't turn him in. If the cops wanted him, they could find him themselves. He was innocent until proven guilty.

But Ryan couldn't stay at our house any more, not now that we knew he was a on the run. Paddy is English. As a pre-Brexit European Union citizen, he had a legal right to live in Spain, but I am American. Harboring a fugitive would jeopardize my immigration status.

As for Angela, she was an adult. She had to make up her own mind about Ryan, but she had to make informed decisions. If Ryan didn't tell Angela about his checkered record, we'd have to do it.

The night dragged on. We went to bed.

I woke up early to see the pilgrim out. Angela was there at the kitchen table, still wearing her party clothes. She'd been crying.

"I can't continue," she said. "I will not see him anymore."

"Thank God," I said. "That's a wise decision. Go home and sleep. We'll talk later."

It was a long day, and a longer afternoon – Ryan slept until 1 p.m., and woke up to a confrontation. He sat in our patio and spun a tale worn smooth with much telling: True love with a doomed girl, 17 years old, addicted to heroin. A vindictive sheriff's deputy. A war-souvenir Nazi pistol, left to Ryan by his uncle in his will. His grandma's last goodbye, just before a midnight run to Canada to catch a plane to Europe. The tale was a thing of beauty, like a Bruce Springsteen ballad.

We paid Ryan his wages, threw in an extra 50. He left that evening, headed west on the Camino de Santiago, a newly credentialed pilgrim. We wished him well, we said, but he couldn't come back to Moratinos. "I'm cool with that," he told us.

Things had solved themselves without any official interference. Ryan was already paying for his sins, wandering the earth like Cain. We weren't going to send him to jail.

I am not sure what Ryan told Angela. I felt guilty for a long time, even though I knew I'd done the right thing. I was angry at Ryan for playing with Angela's heart, and for putting us in that position.

He'd do well on the Camino, I thought. His kind of charm plays well out there.

Somehow, when Ryan passed through Astorga, he met

up with David and Malin. (That's how things work on the Camino.) They had Moratinos and the Peaceable in common, so Ryan told them a colorful tale about fleeing town when Angela's dad threatened him with a shotgun.

The months passed. Ryan finished the Way, then headed south. He stayed in touch with Malin and David; they visited him once at a hippie co-op in Portugal. He was living in a hut made of sticks, Malin said, growing a beard and a forest of marijuana plants.

And now, like a bad penny, he was back.

I was unhappy, but I let myself trust our friends to keep things in line. The welding went off without incident. Angela stayed away in Burgos. Ryan was gone when we got home, but he signed off with a lovely piece of work: a chimney to replace the crumbling ventilation pipe atop our bodega cave, a monumental construction of concrete and stones.

Ryan left a rambling opus behind, written in rhyming couplets. The chimney was a memorial to lost love, he said – a cairn erected over a love lying buried beneath our pueblo, a passion slain by a past that would not let him have a future.

Ryan is a tragic figure, a romantic hero, a Peter Pan, and a jerk. The Camino seems to attract men like him, Lost Boys wandering this Never-Never Land, looking for a home, a family, unconditional love.

On Sunday I saw Pablo at church. He asked if "that boy" was still at our house, and I said no, he'd gone.

"Kids," he said.

I have never seen Pablo out hunting. Someday I will ask him if he owns a shotgun.

9

QUICK AND DIRTY

The galgos settled into our rhythm. Nabi was bolder and a bit crazy. Lulu was tall and shy, and deeply attached to me. Kim sat with them in the barn, on the enormous leaf-green sofa the former owners had left behind. It was wide enough for three: Two skinny galgo girls on either end, legs and tails akimbo, with Kim in the middle, scratching their velvet bellies. The barn was dark and dirty, but the galgos liked it better than the house.

The house was warm, but there were people in there, and closed doors. The galgos did not like to feel closed-in. We gave them time and affection, and lots of food, and slowly they came around. That combination works wonders with all kinds of animals, including pilgrims. Feed them, make sure they're comfortable, show them some attention, and then leave them alone.

Pilgrims sleep very well at our house, even when the heat is not working so well. The salon, the pilgrim bedroom, is a high-gravity place. Pilgrims sleep hard in there, and they dream, too. Big, elaborate, bright visions.

It's a big room, with three single beds. There's a fireplace that's never worked, and a wall covered in bookshelves. If we collect anything it's books. And pictures, and spices. And dogs.

Patrick does not like going for a walk without dogs. He marvels at the number of dogless pilgrims. "What's the point?" he asks them. The pilgrims invariably ask him: "What's a man like you, a philosopher, doing out here in the middle of nowhere?"

Patrick loves that question. "My friend, we are far from the middle of nowhere," he tells them. "This is the middle of Everywhere."

Patrick – Paddy – first came to Spain in the 1960's, one of millions of British holidaymakers who brought the then-wife and kids to the concrete beaches down south. Patrick is an artist, but he sold out early to make a living laying out newspapers. He spent years working for a big London tabloid, and eventually took a job at "Hola!" a celebrity-gossip magazine in Madrid. He helped transform it into an English-language product, and now "Hello!" is a UK institution. Fate and boredom took him over the ocean to The Toledo Blade, a newspaper in Ohio, USA. That's where I met him. I was a reporter and editor there, in charge of religion coverage, and Patrick designed the pages of my section every Friday afternoon.

I was a single mom. I couldn't stay out late on week-nights, but occasionally I'd have a beer with Patrick over at the neighborhood bar. We discovered we both loved Spain, and art, and animals. When I took over art coverage on the paper, Patrick came along to a few show-openings – he knew all about contemporary art, and it was nice having company on cross-country drives to Cleveland, Columbus, Chicago, and Detroit.

We got to know one another. Patrick's girlfriend took a job in Hawaii, and left him with a houseful of pets. He lent me his ferret, Cootie. Back then I spoke passable German, and when breaking news sent me to Germany, Patrick volunteered to stay at my house. The children knew him, and the ferret was already there.

I had a big house. Patrick moved into the spare room. He ended up staying.

My kids – they were teenagers then – called Cootie "the Trojan ferret."

Patrick says things did not really fall out that way, but that's my story, the "quick and dirty." We tell these stories over and over, because pilgrims always ask.

It was in the Toledo years, in 2001, that I finally walked the whole Camino. I could go because Patrick was there, riding herd on the children and animals. He came along to

Spain for the first week or so, walked from Roncesvalles to Logroño, and went back to work.

Patrick hated the Camino. "I did not come here on my holiday to live like a pig," he said after his first night in an albergue. We stayed in little hotels after that. But once he left, my real Camino kicked in. I became a pilgrim. Magical things started to happen.

I arrived early at Najera. I checked in at the albergue, left my bags behind, and took a bus to San Millan de Cogolla, a marvelous off-the-Camino monastic monument. It was San Isidro day, when farmers celebrate their patron saint and priests bless the fields and tractors. I found an English-speaking tour guide, who told me I'd just missed the last bus back to Najera. She interceded. A farmer could take me back, she said, but I'd have to go there in his freshly-blessed tractor.

And so I did. I crammed myself into the cab with a grizzled old guy called Mauricio and his little terrier dog, who jumped up into my arms. I spoke almost no Spanish. Mauricio spoke no English, but I had to make some conversation. The dog was a natural start.

"Your dog is friendly," I said. "What is his name?"

"Peregrino," the man said. Pilgrim.

"Why did you call him that? Did you find him on the Camino?"

"No. I call him that because he smells so bad," Mauricio said, cackling and pinching his nostrils. It took me a minute to translate what he'd said, but then I laughed out loud.

I am not sure when or where on that month-long hike the idea struck me, but I left Spain knowing that I'd really like to live there. Someplace along the Camino, where I could invite pilgrims in for dinner, and hang out in good company. A European country with functional socialism and a spectacular cultural and architectural heritage. Why not?

It turned out Patrick only hated the Camino the first couple of days, when the mud was ankle-deep. He liked the rest of it well enough to go back in 2002 and pick up where he left off, and walk to the end. Then came the volunteer hospitalero phase, when we spent two-week chunks of our summer holidays running pilgrim shelters.

We agreed we'd like to live together along the Camino, but we were too lazy to run our own albergue. I started looking at our financial situation. I shifted things around, made some wily investments.

We studied Spanish at the local university. We spent a month in Mexico in a language immersion program. We got married. Patrick retired. We moved to Pittsburgh for a while, Una adopted us. We learned to live on a single pension check, and invested the rest.

I took a leave from my job in June of 2006, and left Una with my cousin Barbara. We flew to Spain, leased a car, and drove from one volunteer gig to another, staying at places along the Caminos that we knew had potential. Two weeks here, two weeks there, seeing how the town treated foreigners, getting a feel for transportation, education, and cultural options. We talked to other expatriates, sought out Camino pioneers, and poked around backwater castles and convents in the days between.

It was an unforgettable summer. It was the summer we found Moratinos, and the house that became The Peaceable.

10

THE DARK SIDE OF THE LIGHT

Rafferty, my friend from Glasgow, has worked with pilgrims for years. He's been a pilgrim himself, but he's never got his head around The Peaceable. "Running an albergue is one thing," he says, "but you let the buggers into your house. I could never do that. Ah doont know how you do it."

We let pilgrims stay in our house with us. It's a big place, and they only use a couple of rooms, and we don't have pilgrims every day. We keep a bathroom for ourselves, and no one is allowed in our bedroom or office. Almost all pilgrims are decent, low-maintenance people. We have room to spare, and if we didn't give them a place to stay, they'd end up out in the rain. If there are not too many of them, pilgrims can be a lot of fun.

I'm not saying it's easy. People call us "saints" and "angels," but those beings are too easily dismissed. If we were supernatural, this would be easy-peasy. If this was easy and risk-free, everyone would do it. We do it because we believe in power of pilgrimage to transform peoples' lives. Because we like the company. Because it's fulfilling, much of the time. If we didn't like it, we'd stop.

Problems are built into the Camino concept. Pilgrimage is not engineered to work in a Capitalist economy. You can be a pilgrim, and you can be a born-and-raised consumer. You just can't be both at the same time.

Camino has a Gospel vibe, and people from everywhere figure that anything Christian has got to come free of charge – maybe because the Catholic church supposedly has billions of bucks in the basement, or because Jesus' grace comes for free.

The Camino is undeniably Christian. When you walk the Camino, no matter how you feel about religion, you join the righteous. You become a pilgrim, a historically sanctioned person. You strip down your possessions to only what fits in your backpack, and you set out on a journey surrounded by churches, crucifixes, weeping virgins and donation boxes.

People raised in consumer economies quickly find out that Spain is beautiful, the people are great, and having nothing has its perks. Pilgrims can stay for almost nothing at old convents and schoolhouses. The beds are creaky, the plumbing is grotty, but hey – it's practically free, and it's all put there for pilgrims! If a traveler leaves nothing in the donation box, nobody notices. You can travel, eat, drink, and sleep for free. What's not to like?

Back at its 13th century peak, the church — the Christians — subsidized the Camino. The noble pilgrim persona, the scruffy housing, the lifestyle, all are supplied by church tradition. Medieval kings and nobles supported the monasteries that supported the pilgrims. Monks went out and begged around the neighborhood for funds to feed the holy travelers, they grew the livestock and grain and fruit and vegetables that went into the cooking pot. The pilgrimage had its own economy behind it.

Nowadays, though, albergues are on their own. There are no kings or monks or public funds to hold the place together – just the nickels and dimes in the collection box. Pilgrims don't know this, or they don't choose to. Spanish pilgrims especially cherish the idea that the church, or the government, or a foundation provides the funding, and pilgrims are entitled to a free ride. Anyone who asks them to pay their way "doesn't have the Camino spirit."

The Camino is built on an outdated premise, a spiritual economy – but it exists in real time, in a free market, with taxes and bills, fees and overhead. Albergue owners start out warm and idealistic, but soon feel the cold fingers of Capitalism closing 'round their wallets. The Mario Brothers were like that. They stayed at our house, slept, washed, ate, and drank, and paid what they said they would charge their pilgrims, once they got started: Five euros per person, per day. It's no wonder things did not work out well. They did not mean to take advantage of us, but in the end we felt exploited. And peevish, and a lot less-than Christian. Halfway through April, Patrick told the Italians we were all for their albergue idea, but they'd have to find someplace else to live. We couldn't subsidize their dreams anymore.

There were some hard feelings for a while, but in the fullness of time they saw for themselves just how expensive it is to serve a customer base with a built-in percentage of freeloaders.

It wasn't easy for the Italians. They spent a lot of time in Palencia chasing down permits, and at the job site, waiting for carpenters and plumbers, welders and electricians who showed up when they got around to it. Bruno lost a lot of weight. Kim introduced him to the galgos, and as their project continued, Bruno too spent quiet moments on the dog sofa in the barn, telling his troubles to fellow sufferers.

Una took a shine to Bruno. When we walked the dogs en masse each morning in the fields, she often excused herself, and instead lingered at the work site. She supervised demolition of the old straw-and-timber roofs and the maze of walls that cut the house into tiny rooms. She'd seen us do that. She had experience. Chasing through the fields was getting beyond her.

Progress came in fits and starts. Because they were converting an old house into a place for public use, they had to meet requirements from every level of Spanish bureaucracy. An archaeologist came to inspect the site, to ensure no ancient ruins were lurking beneath the surface. He told us the *tumberon* – a big knobby hill in the fields outside town – was an unexcavated Neolithic tomb. There are dozens of them in the district, he said. We marveled pleasingly.

"Why don't you excavate?" Patrick asked.

"We have all the flints and stone axes and potsherds we need," the guy answered. "It's best to just leave it alone. There's nothing new up there."

Just something very, very old.

There was a monastery near here, too, a very long time ago – a little place on the road between here and Terradillos de los Templarios. There's nothing left of it now, but it was called St. John, run by the Order of St. John – the Templar Knights. Three of our neighbors have rough-hewn stone watering troughs in their back gardens, hauled home by their ancestors once that monastery was finally burned down and abandoned. The troughs are full of junk now, or weeds, but if you take a good look you will see the human shape cut into the rock. They're sarcophagi. Tombs, where the bodies of long-ago knights or abbots moldered away.

There is no stone here. Buildings and walls are made of rammed earth or adobe bricks, covered-over with coatings of mud and whitewash. Building with what's to hand is labor-intensive, and maintaining it is a drag. No one uses those methods any more. Modern bricks and concrete are cheaper and last much longer, so adobe buildings are abandoned, doomed to slow erosion.

Stone and brick were used only for important public buildings, castles, palaces, or churches. In Moratinos, the church is the oldest building in town, the only one with a stone foundation. The church is old. And the bodegas. No one can say how old they are, or even how old this town is.

Bodegas are wine storage caves, dug into the sides of a hill alongside the plaza, a hill called "el Castillo," the castle. There's never been a castle in Moratinos. These are caves, man-made tunnels leading down to cellars, sitting rooms, wine presses – forever the same steady cool temperature. A hundred years ago, when more than 100 people lived in Moratinos, there were 21 of these cellars, handed down and expanded across generations along with houses, fields, animals, and orchards. Now that immigration and tractors have transformed Castilian agriculture, no one needs a bodega any more. Only ten of them are still intact.

The bodegas are the first things pilgrims see when they

walk into town, and often as not they wonder if Hobbits live inside them. The doors are locked, and the roofs of several have collapsed, leaving dangerous maws in the earth. The pilgrims, invincible, clamber up and over the hill to marvel at the views from the top.

We have a bodega. It came with our house. We had it added to the title deed when we bought the place. Before us, it did not exist, legally. Before, everybody just knew which one belonged to whom.

We keep a modest store of wine inside, and spare tools. Ours is one of the largest and tallest in town, and still has a wine press at one end, and three big barrels in a niche near the entrance. We should to do something with it, make it useful somehow, maybe let pilgrims see inside, to satisfy their natural curiosity.

We left it open once, accidentally – just overnight – back when it was still stacked full of homemade wine gone bad. Pilgrims got in there and enjoyed themselves. They left candy wrappers and water bottles. They tried their luck with the stock of ancient vinegar. They left behind toilet paper, and feces, and urine.

I put a solid lock on the door. I am not saint enough to happily clean up shit, or to forgive that kind of ugliness.

I have a long way to go.

11

HOME

There's a fat little book in our house full of comments left by the pilgrims who've stayed. It is not compelling reading. In many languages the pilgrims say "thank you," they say "great food," or "I slept so well," or "God bless you, saints and angels."

The word they use most is "home."

"You opened your home," they say. "It's so homey here." "A home away from home." "I felt like I was right at home."

The Peaceable really is a home. It is thousands of miles from where my family lives and where my ancestors are buried, but I have never felt nearly so comfortable and settled-in anywhere else. In this tiny town in the middle of a huge plain, in a country where I do not speak the language, I found the place that speaks to my spirit.

The sun shines with a fierce white light, and the south-facing patio grabs up every ray. The barn and house and back-garden wall dug into a hillside, sheltered from the wind. Whoever built this place was a genius – or geniuses. It took generations to build. It went up in stages, over centuries. You can see it in the lay of the brick, and the layout – it started out as a sheepfold, and morphed into a simple home for a farmer and her family, cows and donkeys, mules, and tools. Low, dark rooms for keeping warm, tiny windows to keep out the wind, the kitchen set back across the patio, to keep fires from igniting the barn or the beds.

When we bought it there still was a watering trough in the middle of the patio, and the barn was knee-deep in rotted straw. The main house had three whitewashed bedrooms and a rummage-sale's worth of mismatched furniture. There was no plumbing. Electricity was a wire tacked up on the wall. I have seen brighter, safer Christmas trees.

It took years to make it ours, years of frustration and wasted time, tears and fury and even a lawsuit. We lived in the tiny kitchen, slept in a storage room alongside, washed and relieved ourselves in a primitive bathroom under a tin roof. Throughout all that time, the pilgrims came. They did not complain. There was nowhere else for them to sleep in Moratinos.

The builders did not think we'd last. They thought we'd give up and go home soon, so we were gleefully ripped-off, scoffed-at, abandoned, and ignored. We almost despaired a few times, but usually some special pilgrim came along and helped us out.

Tomas from Croatia was a shipwright who became a soldier in the Bosnian war. He did terrible things then, and walked the Camino to atone for them. He worked from dawn to dark with a roll-up cigarette dangling from his lip. He could swing a scythe, patch plaster, and render adobe walls using a paint sprayer. He ate anything we put in front of him, and drank himself to sleep at night. We paid him every Saturday, when he biked into Sahagun and played the slot machines at Bar Sergio. Kim was his confessor. When he left us, he gave me an electric-pink orchid plant as a thank-you gift. He gave Patrick a Venus Fly Trap.

Anselmo helped us, too, and Jesus. They were forest rangers from Cadiz, laid-off in summer, traveling the Camino as hospitaleros and work-for-food laborers. They barked for us in Spanish at builders who did not show up and roofers who walked off halfway through the job. Milo, a young, 7-foot-tall art historian from Czech Republic, helped me lay a tile floor in the storage room. It was a disaster, but we enjoyed ourselves.

They stayed for weeks at a time, did heavy work, left their handprints in the mortar. Some of them still come back. Frederic has been stopping here for six or seven years now – he is a wiry little Frenchman with a startling resemblance to Popeye the Sailor. He's a little slow, victim of a shipyard accident in Marseilles, a former drug addict whose miracle transformation was wrought by the L'Arche Community. When he first arrived here I didn't want to let him in. He was bleary-eyed, had prison tattoos on his knuckles, and had obviously been sleeping rough. Patrick said "give him a chance."

There's another class of traveling man, embodied by Antonio from Portugal. He tramps up and down the Camino, sleeping rough or for free in donativo albergues, saying "please," asking nice, taking what he can get. He doesn't do a lick of work, but he carries several changes of clothes, a sleeping bag, and jacket to suit the season. The Camino is his home. He works the system.

After a hot meal and a couple glasses of tinto, Antonio leans back in his chair and looks over the room. He waits until Patrick goes away. He leans in.

"Rebekah," he says, confidentially. "Do you have a good rain poncho? I need one. It's going to rain."

Truth is, I often have extra ponchos. Pilgrims are always leaving things behind, lightening their loads. Antonio renews his belongings in "lost and found" boxes all up and down the trail. Antonio asks for coats, knives, shoelaces, even hiking boots. He complains bitterly when we don't have his size.

"This isn't a boot store," Patrick says. Antonio laughs his

wheezy laugh. "Patrick," he says, leaning in close. "Rebekah only gave me ten euro."

Antonio is a bum, but we have never turned him away. His wheedling is irritating. If there's any money left in the donativo box, he'll help himself. A lot of people slam their doors in his face. Maybe they're right to do so. But Antonio's an authentic Camino character, playing a time-honored role. He's got as much right to the trail as anybody.

The pilgrims who stay overnight are geared into the Camino machine. Their job is walking, or biking – following this program, this trail, this time-honored pathway. They are on their way to Santiago de Compostela. We believe in what they are doing, we support them. I believe the pilgrimage road is a key to peace in the world. Wonderful, unifying things happen here that don't happen anywhere else. Pilgrims come here to find God, or answers, or peace. They end up finding one another.

The Peaceable is a stop along the way for a few of them, another page in their story. I get to meet these holy people as they pass. When I care to look, I often see God in them, in every kind of disguise.

Some of them finish their journey and come back and stay a few days. Some come here on purpose, to help with a specific project. Others come once in a blue moon, just to see us. They step into our rhythm. They relax into the work, and let go of a lot of things that hem them in back home.

Home. They come here because we don't ask them for much. We feed them, and sometimes we drink with them, work alongside them, and invite them to come along to the Roman Villa or the next village, or to Sunday church.

And for people who feel homeless, this place is attractive. It looks to them like home, and they want to stay around, whether or not we need another person here.

Rosario, an elderly, spry lady from Madrid, stayed here for two days, recovering from bad blisters. She made delicious ensaladilla Rusa, and salmorejo. She couldn't move around much, so she bossed the other pilgrims from her kitchen chair. While she stayed, everyone made up his bed, folded his blankets, washed his dishes and swept the floor after breakfast. When her third morning rolled around, Rosario packed up her things, kissed us on both cheeks, and declared her intentions.

"My children are grown up, my husband is gone, I have no grandchildren. My apartment is much too big for just me. I am bored, I have no function. When I finish the Camino, I will go back and sell my apartment. I am coming back here and live. This is a home. I really love it here. I will cook, and help with the pilgrims."

Patrick and I looked at one another. We laughed nervously.
"You are very generous," I said. "But you must talk with your children first. They need you. And if they've never walked the Camino, they will never understand."

Rosario stood for a moment, blinking in the morning sun.

"You are saints," she said. "You only say that because you are good. A lot of people would just say yes."

We said goodbye. We didn't see her again.

12

FIRE IN THE HOLE

The sun came out. Kim went to Barcelona to try out convent life for a couple of weeks. She and one of the Mario Brothers had picked up a hitch-hiking nun a few weeks before, a pilgrim who'd finished the Way and was heading home. Kim is far from Catholic, but one thing led to another. The nun invited Kim over to visit, so Kim went.

Repairmen came in turns to fix the water heater and washing machine and the little-kitchen pipes. Everything goes at once, it seems. Repairmen, though, only come when they're ready.

Nights were still cold, but spring brought us out from our caves. I started some quicklime in the big blue barrel in the barn, mixed some concrete, and put the blown-down tiles back up on the perimeter walls. We cleaned out the sheep trough, started a window-box of carrots, planted Brussels sprouts and peas. It was too early, but I did it anyway. Countless seeds are sacrificed each year to my enthusiasm.

A hobo came to the back gate while I was working. Patrick took him inside and gave him coffee and fried eggs and mandarin oranges. Patrick brought Nabi Dog into the back garden. She met the chickens and Murphy cat and paid them little mind, but when Patrick started cutting up firewood with the chainsaw, Nabi asked to go back to the barn.

The Italians came back to town. They moved to a little flat in Sahagun. Their progress was slow. Patrick and I were alone in the house again, for the first time since early January. For hermits, we were very busy.

On a bright Saturday morning, the church bells rang the "all hands on deck" ring. Patrick hiked down to see what the news might be: it was tree-trimming day. We gathered up rakes and tarpaulins and headed downtown.

Tractors were converted to front-end loaders, and some of the men already were lifted up into the branches of the plaza trees, bashing with hatchets, slashing with chainsaws.

The plaza is ringed with *chopos,* a particular kind of cypress tree whose branches grow flat and leafy. If properly trained, they intertwine and form a dappled green canopy in summer. In winter, though, the skyward-growing canes must be cut back hard. Cutting them down and bundling them up is a big job, but it can be done in a day if enough people pitch in. This year we started very late, but the cold snap would work to our advantage, Juan said.

Moratinos' plaza isn't much. There's the porch side of the

church, and the old schoolhouse-town hall, and the walls of peoples' houses on each side. What once was a boggy communal cow yard was, sometime in the 1960s, paved-over with concrete slabs. The spring was channeled into a hydrant where pilgrims fill their water bottles, and *chopo* trees were planted for shade, to break the hard angles of concrete. A slapdash triangle of dirt served as a community flower garden where a couple of fig trees and rose bushes struggle to survive. Zinnias raise their heads in summer, but no one takes much care, because nobody really owns it.

Once a year though, usually in late winter, everyone comes out to put the place in order. Patrick and I pitch in, even though we're not very useful. The men chopped branches, while we who lacked tractors and power tools simply raked out the flower garden onto the canvas and hauled the waste to the compost pile. I cut back the rose bushes, maybe too far. Nobody cared, long as we showed up and did our bit, and stayed out of the way of falling branches. It was good fun out in the bright cold air, picking up sticks, binding up big bundles with baling twine.

At the end of the day, the bundles, valuable winter fuel, were carefully divided among the households. Most old houses still use wood- or straw-fired under-floor tunnel furnaces to heat large sections of the homestead. The bundled branches burn long and slow, and they fit right into the fire-hole beneath the porch or the stairs. They call these furnaces "glorias," and 1,800 years ago, the Romans who lived here used the same technology to heat their villas. It's perfectly suited in a land where tons of surplus straw are threshed every harvest, and people in the winter have nothing better to do than chop up sticks and straw for keeping warm.

We had one of those gloria furnaces under our little kitchen when we first moved in. Like much of our house, it was built by amateurs. We stuffed it full of straw one nippy afternoon, opened the flue on the chimney, and lit it up. I waited inside with my feet flat on the tiles. Patrick ran out and looked up – Yes! Smoke was pouring from the chimney! And yes! The floor got hot, too. Patrick and I sat in the lowdown Naugahyde club chairs the old owners had left behind, and gloated at one another. We had a toasty warm gloria of our own!

But little curls of white smoke rose up from the cracks between the tiles underfoot. They raced upward, flattened along the ceiling, and blossomed out to coat the room grey. The gloria pipe beneath the floor was cracked. The smoke took the quickest path upward, right through the floor and into the little kitchen. If we stayed in there we'd be warm alright. We'd soon be smoked like a couple of kippers.

We opened all the windows, shouted some bad words,

waved newspapers, dragged the smoldering straw from the hatch and stamped it out in the entryway. For weeks the kitchen smelled like a half-smoked cigar.

We had no need of gloria fuel, so we pitched our share of firewood bundles onto the wagon meant for Pilar, whose husband has early-onset Alzheimer's disease. Pilar's family couldn't help anymore with community chores, but the community helped them anyway. At the end of that Saturday, they had enough fuel in their barn for most of the next winter.

Once the plaza was shaven and swept, everyone went home for a nap. And once the sun went down, we reassembled at Arturo's bodega for the "merienda," a snack.

A post-tree-trim merienda is no snack. It's a Rabelaisian banquet, a feast held inside a darksome wine-storage cave. Arturo climbed a ladder and hooked jumper cables to a wire along the wall. The single lightbulb inside flickered to life. We entered through a door in the hillside and settled ourselves on long benches around a table laid with pitchers of rough wine made right there. Great plates of tiger shrimp were passed, then lemon slices, then lettuce leaves, sliced tomatoes, carrots, onions, and a bidon of superb olive oil. Crusty bread came by – everyone tore off what they wanted, and passed the loaf along.

The women carried food and place-settings from their houses on the plaza over to the bodegas, the men turned the meat on the coals. It was lamb, chops cut from a black-faced baby butchered that morning in Justi's barn. They put the grilled kidneys and liver slices on a little plate and set it at Patrick's place, because everyone knows Patrick likes those. The chops went onto chipped white platters, and made the rounds of the table. We were ten or twelve people. More meat was passed than could have fit on the bones of a single suckling lamb, but who am I to question a miracle of providence?

We talked about cecina, a dried sausage made usually of beef, but sometimes of wild boar, or venison, and sometimes horse, donkey, or mule. People cured whatever meat they had back in the old days, they hung it to cure on a hook inside the chimney. We talked about our crumbling church tower, and how best to secure the bells up there, how the stairs and ladders inside were dangerously riddled with woodworm. What should we do? I posited a staircase made of steel, brought in sections on a truck and welded up in place. Patrick and I had seen the very thing in a church in Medina de Rioseco. Everyone agreed that was a crazy idea.

I'd gotten used to being dismissed that way. I didn't let it bother me much. In that case, the passage of time proved me right.

The boys passed homemade "white lightning," and a song or two was sung. By 10:30 p.m. I wriggled free from my corner bench. I did my womanly duty by collecting everyone's empty plates. Outside the door I scraped the scraps into waiting basins. I stacked the empties. I scrubbed down the sharp knives at the hydrant in the plaza, and with shivering hands I wrapped the blades in newspaper and left them inside the front door of Remedios' house. I slipped up the silent street to home, one pocket full of bones for my dogs, the other full of shrimp-shells for my hens.

I started thinking about walking.

It happens every spring, and it's only natural, seeing as we live along a pilgrim path. I talk almost every day with pilgrims, I see the excitement and unity and fun they're having, and I remember what a wonder my first Camino was. Daily dog-walks aren't enough, even really long ones. I want to get out and stretch my muscles, do some distance. I'd done shorter Caminos, week-long hikes – I'd even written some guides -- but I wanted to do The Big One again, to see what's new, what had changed.

The Camino is magical. But when magic becomes part of your day-to-day, you can lose touch. I wanted to feel that On The Road pilgrim juju again.

It had been almost ten years since I'd walked the whole

thing. This was a holy year. And now Kim was with us – Kim could watch the house, drive the car, take care of business. I was free to go. I wouldn't have to worry.

My first Camino took years to achieve. It required a leave from work, complicated childcare arrangements, transatlantic flights, and big money. This time the usual starting point was just a four-hour train-ride away. I spoke the language now, more or less. I knew the trail, I knew a good number of the innkeepers along the way. I could even stop at home halfway and do my laundry.

I hunted up my backpack, ordered some hiking socks from Amazon, and made out a pilgrim credential for myself. I asked Little Angela if she wanted to go. She liked the idea, but she didn't think she had the physical stamina. Besides, she'd be working right through June. Her mom Maribel had always wanted to walk the Way, but it would take a whole month. They had a crop in the field, and she was reader at church, and there was no one else at home to look after Pablo and Fran, her handicapped brother. Someday, Maribel said, the Lord would make it possible.

Maribel was older than me, but she was a strong hiker. We often did a two-hour "rally" to Terradillos in the late afternoons, and on weekends when Little Angela was home from Burgos. Maribel walked fast, and never stopped chattering the whole way. Six weeks of that would certainly bring me to repentance. Pablo would probably forbid it, anyway. Women belong at home, they cannot be left wandering over the countryside.

Kim came back, unconverted, from Barcelona. I caught the train eastward the following day. I went alone. My husband approved. I had no standing crops, no promises to keep. This Camino would be different from the last one, I knew it.

13

INVISIBLE OLD GOD

It was easy. No big deal. No big excitement.

I met Oscar, a very large man from Asturias, who didn't make it very far.

I met Hideo, a young Japanese pilgrim who'd walked from LePuy in France and was ready to go home. He had found his calling on the trail. He was going to join the Dominicans, he said, but his plane ticket wasn't good for another month. He had almost no money. He'd just have to keep walking until then. I asked him to pray for me.

I developed an impressive blister, a long, skinny one, all along the edge of my left foot. Pilgrims get to know their feet intimately. Their blisters have names. I called this one "Mack the Knife."

I prayed a lot, I went to Mass whenever I could find one; I visited churches when they were open, and occasionally sought out the key-holders to village churches I knew had some art treasure inside. I had enough Spanish, I knew how to ask nicely. I invited other pilgrims to come along. I tried not to come off like a know-it-all, but I really was by then pretty expert in things Camino. I made some friends.

We bandaged one another's battered toes, and watched each other's valuables while we went into the bushes to "shake hands with the president." A Czech girl named Zuzana walked with me a while. She walked for the sake of her mother's health. Her mother had Stage 4 cancer, and Zuzana wanted St. James to work a miracle.

Rory joined us outside Burgos. He was an Anglican youth minister in an urban English wasteland, trapped in a bad marriage. He was even more self-absorbed than the usual pilgrim.

The albergue at the Monastery of San Juan de Ortega was drafty and cold, only just reopened for Holy Week. Deep in the night, in the darkness of my bunkbed, I felt a many-legged spider skitter across the top of my hand. I slapped down hard, I got him! But not before he bit me. My hand went incandescent, I could feel it swelling as the venom ran hot up my arm. My breath shortened. I am terribly allergic to all kinds of things. Anaphylactic shock can kill me quick, but somehow I did not feel fearful. Should I wake up someone? Should I cry out? I waited too long. Darkness closed in. "This may be it," I thought to myself. "Maybe I am dying now."

I think I just fell back to sleep.

The next morning was a sunny Palm Sunday – appropriate

enough for someone whose left hand was Mickey Mouse-sized. The spider carcass was there atop my sleeping bag, proof that I hadn't just dreamed it all. There was nothing to do but keep going. On the way to Burgos a village church discharged its load of worshipers. Skillful children braided palm crosses into the straps of our backpacks. Rory and Zuzana were obviously sparking. I let them move off ahead.

I walked alone for the next couple of weeks. Sometimes I wondered what the hell I was doing out there.

People talked to me, and I listened. I gave away my maps and bandages and fizzy vitamin packets, and now and then rubbed someone's aching knee or shoulder until the muscles let go and relaxed. If someone asked, I told them what I knew.

No one did those things for me. I ministered, but was not ministered-to. I simply did not connect with anyone.

My first Camino came with a tight little group of suddenly intimate friends, including a beautiful Catholic priest from Holland. He became a confidante, and he is a great friend to this day. But that second Camino, I told my soul to God himself, and God must have heard me, because God kept me going. I had enough spirituality and caring to share with others, and enough left over for me. But not enough to make me feel all warm and charged-up and Camino-y.

It didn't feel good. I wanted that nice fuzzy fellowship

feeling you get from friends. I wanted a person, another pilgrim, but all I got was invisible old God.

I stopped at Moratinos for Easter, but I took off walking soon as my laundry was done. I was in Pilgrim Mode, and didn't want to lose momentum. On a bright sunny morning at the Cruz de Ferro I laid down a stone for my cousin Michelle, who'd died much too young a couple of weeks before. At that sacred place where the veil is so thin, I let her go. I cried like a baby.

A busload of Belgian tourists snapped my picture.

Nearby was a much-pierced pilgrim with a portable stereo, blasting speed-metal music.

A group of ten Spanish executives, on the sacred trail for a "team-building exercise," left a trail of litter in their wake.

Just over the mountain in El Acebo I learned about another trail. A wise innkeeper called Jaime told me about Peñalba del Camino, a remote shrine above The Valley of Silence. It connects to the Camino de Invierno, "the Winter Camino," a newly marked alternative Way. It was very tough, the man said. Mountain trails at first. Long stretches of mountain between stops.

He had me at "Silence." Solitude. An escape from speed-metal knuckleheads!

I had a lot of second thoughts, but I followed the alternative path. It was deep green, full of birdsong and blooming cherry trees. I met no other pilgrims. It was the toughest two days of walking I have ever done on any camino, and I did the zany things you do after hours alone. I talked to myself, and the trees and birds. I thanked the sardines in the tin for giving their all so I could have lunch. I sang songs out loud, and hoped I was not lost.

I drank from a cattle trough on a mountaintop. There wasn't anything higher up to trickle down into that spring, so I thought it was safe. I made it to Las Medullas at sundown, utterly exhausted.

The following day landed me at the regional hospital at O Barco de Valdeorras, my innards scoured by giardia bacteria. I thought my Camino was over. Patrick hopped a train west, sought me out, and hauled my feverish carcass up to the luxury parador hotel in Monforte de Lemos. I basted for hours in a bathtub of hot, bubbly water, and slept for days in a huge bed with starched sheets. I do not remember it well, but I got better. Patrick walked on with me for a day into the beauty of rural Galician spring: skittering lambs, bread loaves the size of sofa pillows, fresh cheese bought in the farmyard, wide rivers, and hollow trees buzzing with bees.

Alone again, I missed a waymark outside Lalin, and wandered for hours in a pine plantation. Rain drizzled down. I finally flagged a tractor and asked the farmer for a ride into town. History repeated itself, but this time there was no smelly Peregrino dog. I stood on the axle behind the driver's open seat, my poncho-tails flapping romantically behind me... at least until I remembered Isadora Duncan and her fatal scarf.

I enjoy my own company. I do not usually mind being alone. I don't have many intimates. Even when I am low I don't call on my friends, much as I love them. I am a fundamentally alone person, I have learned to live happily with a chilly independence that many find unbecoming in a woman.

But at the base of me, in my heart, is a furnace full of God. This is the way he made me, and it is beautiful just the way it is. That is what that long walk taught me.

Mine was not a Big Fun Camino, but it was important. Compared to 2001, there were many, many more places to eat and drink and sleep, many more opportunities to spend money, and a lot fewer opportunities to connect with other pilgrims. I felt I should have met and known some of them, but they chose instead to seal themselves off behind mobile phones or media headgear, their ears and senses full of music or books or something else they'd brought along from home.

There wasn't so much togetherness, or sharing across the tables. Wine still worked its magic in the evenings. Friendships and flirtation still flowered on the trail, but not for me. In nine years the path and the pilgrims had changed out of recognition. And so had I.

The final day before Santiago I engineered my morning walk just so, carefully timed to arrive for the noon Pilgrim Mass. The morning was misty, the farmers forked fragrant hay into tall wagons pulled by oxen. I pounded along to the city that rose up in the distant valley, my hiking staff bumping the ground. The minutes ticked by. The city didn't seem to get much nearer.

I entered the aging suburbs of spalled concrete, ruined houses, and wide detours around half-finished highway ramps. I stopped at a grubby bar for a shot of caffeine. I could hear the cathedral bells tolling the hour. Eleven. I was cutting this close. I paid, I left, I moved fast down the sidewalk, into the traffic. I didn't want to have to wait until tomorrow's pilgrim Mass. This one was mine!

But the way was too long, the bells tolled the quarter-hours now, and it became clear that no, the cathedral was still way up on top that hill, and I was just too far away.

Damn this, I thought. This camino was just such a goddamn disappointment. I started to cry. I was beaten, dirty, and sad.

The cathedral bells banged out noon. There was a church right there, a hulking black Romanesque pile alongside a creek called Rio Sar, just on the edge of the old Santiago city limits. Might as well go in there for a minute, I thought. Take a break in the dark.

A lady at the gate stamped my credential and told me a busload of tourists had just arrived. Just my luck, I thought. But Sar welcomed me. It was a monastery once, long ago – the cloister a splendid garden now, full of pansies and daisies. There was a schoolyard on the other side of the convent wall, the laughter and shouts of children filled that quiet place with joy. This was a parish church, a school. The ancient monastery was still alive, serving the working-class neighborhood around it.

They were singing inside the church. I stepped into the dark and let my eyes adjust, let myself listen to the music reverberating off the heavy stones. I knew the tune. I knew the words. They were singing, in English, "Amazing Grace."

The tourists were a Canadian church group traveling with their own priest. A man patted the pew beside him, stood up to help me peel off my pack. Lou, he said, from Saskatoon.

I cried right through their Mass. It became my Mass, really, in my church, provided in my native tongue by my patient, loving Father.

I dragged myself into Santiago de Compostela in time for lunch. I was scorched and dry, ready to go home.

14

PATRICK SHAN'T

Moratinos turned green. The trees blossomed, the house next door opened up. The neighbors brought along the old man back from Basque Country.

I never learned his name, but I knew he was Pablo's father, Little Angela's grandfather. He had to be 90. He'd grown up in that tumbledown house before it started tumbling down. He'd plowed these fields behind a team of mules, he'd served in Franco's army during the Spanish Civil War, and now he was bent and frail in his lawn chair. He didn't let himself be confined to the patio. He liked being out along the street, where he could see people and say hello.

He didn't hear so well, but he was still plenty sharp. Patrick hauled a lawn chair down there sometimes and sat with him. He liked Patrick. I don't know what they found to talk about, but the old guy seemed to enjoy being back in his home, even if he only had a foreigner to listen to his stories.

He lived with his daughter in an apartment in Vittoria, because that's what old or infirm people do. They live with their daughters, or sisters, or mothers. Extended families are strong still in Spain, and even though social services and medical care are socialized, those systems take for granted every patient has women enough to help him get along.

Patrick had a minor operation at the hospital that May, he had to stay overnight. There was perfectly competent nursing care, but it wasn't applied in a way I recognized. Because I was "the patient's family," I was expected to attend to his basic needs – walk Patrick to the bathroom, comb his hair, even bring in his meals. People without relatives or friends can hire a bedside helper through the hospital social services office to do these jobs, for very little money. The helpers are usually eastern European immigrant women with big families to support. These ladies are looked-down upon with particular scorn. Not having relatives is sad, but having to hire a foreigner is pathetic. Relying on hospital nursing care and food service is beyond the pale.

I see it as six degrees of institutionalized sexism, but I am a woman, and a foreigner. My opinion means nothing.

I am not a gifted nurse, but I didn't have much choice. I gave Patrick his pre-operation pill in the morning, wheeled him into his wheelchair, and rolled him down to the surgery. We were right on time, as you'd expect of people who spent decades meeting deadlines.

Patrick was first to arrive, so he went in first. I waited for hours while the "procedure" happened.

To calm myself, I prayed with a rosary. I was raised by evangelical Protestants, and rosaries are not part of my faith tradition, but I'd adapted over time. I find the repetitive rhythm of whispered prayers calming and contemplative, a great way to pass time in waiting areas. Rosaries are deeply respected in Spain. Carry one on the bus or train, and tattooed tough guys sometimes offer their seats. It's not all about religion, it's about personal space, and safety. Rosary users may look devout and holy, but they may also be crazy. Onlookers keep a safe distance, just in case.

But I can't pray forever. The respect only lasts until I put the beads away.

The waiting room was dingy tiles and tattered magazines, but no blaring television or screaming babies, thank God. It was crowded with families. When Tia Maria goes in for surgery, apparently the entire family turns out for the occasion, dressed in their Sunday best. I was quickly identified as an English speaker, so three or four youngsters were pressed to practice their schoolroom English on me.

"Hallo, madam. How are joo?" they asked in turn. When I answered, they hid behind their hands.

One little girl introduced herself as Ana, "a pupil of the advanced class." She showed me the contents of her father's wallet. She held each photograph up before the matching relative in the plastic chairs along the wall. "Here is Grandmother," she said in English. "Here is Uncle." "This is my brother. He is name Nano."

"Where is your father?" I asked her. "He is in the doctor," Ana answered gravely, "but a photograph is here. I have his wallet." Ana sat in the seat next to mine. Nano settled his grubby self on my lap, much like Murphy Cat would do. Ana showed me her dad's driver's license, his work ID, his credit cards. She laid them out on the table top, and her cousin put them in rows. A roomful of strangers watched with nary a word about identity theft or personal privacy. The children laid out the money in the wallet, too: Twenty-two euros and forty-five cents, counted-up in English. I was impressed. I gave grandma a thumbs-up sign. The family beamed. The entire waiting room beamed.

A nurse leaned into the room and called out Patrick's name. I jumped up and followed her through the swinging doors.

In the next room, Patrick was knocked out cold on a table, covered with a sheet. He looked like a beached tuna, but the nurse said he was fine, he'd wake up in a little while. Meantime, the doctor swept in, the doctor who'd done the "exploration."

"You are English," he said, looking at his clipboard.

"Patrick is English," I said. "I am American. From the United States."

"You speak English. I speak English too," he said. He'd apparently studied in England, his accent was Midlands upper-class. "I shall tell you about this operation."

Patrick was going to be OK, he said. There was nothing permanently wrong, but he'd have to change his habits. No more bacon or ham, no more fatty pork or sausages.

"No problem. He doesn't eat much of that now," I said.

"Someone has eaten something in the past to create this infirmity," the doctor said, peering at me over the tops of his glasses. "Or perhaps he has drunk something? Mister O'Gara takes alcohol, no?"

"He surely does," I said.

"And so he shall change," the doctor said. He flipped a page on the clipboard.

"From this day on, Mister O'Gara shan't take orujo. He shan't take brandy, nor whiskey, nor gin. He shan't take spirituous liquors," the surgeon said. I smiled to myself. Patrick would love this. Too bad he was unconscious.

I thought for a minute. Shan't. Was the doctor saying the hard stuff was now utterly forbidden, or just inadvisable?

"Are you saying he should not drink liquor, or he cannot drink liquor?" I asked.

The doctor stood up straight and looked at me with hard eyes. "I am speaking English, madam," he snapped. "Mister O'Gara shan't take spirits. It is clear."

"Yes sir," I said. "What about wine?"

"Wine is healthy. Wine is good," he said. "Wine is not spirituous."

I thought about all this for a moment, and realized how much I'd enjoy a glass of something just then. The doctor gave me a handful of papers, the nurse led me back out to the waiting room, and I felt a great wave of relief roll over me. Patrick was OK. I could take him home, once he woke up. I sat down and felt myself relax.

Then I started to weep.

The waiting families went silent. They must have thought the news was bad, that my patient hadn't made it through, and I was there alone, without a family to help me.

I felt a hand touch my knee. Nano put a tissue into my hand. In front of me was Ana, and in her hand was a candy.

"Don't cry, Inglesa," she said in Castellano. "Take a candy. It will be alright."

When we got home Patrick was crabby, but the dogs were ecstatic. Kim had assembled the new patio table and chairs, and had a full-size dinner laid out, al fresco.

Kim makes spectacular salads, and I cannot understand

why lettuce, onion, and tomato are so much better-looking and tasty when she puts them together. I can vacuum and mop and wipe, and the house won't sparkle and shine the same way it does for Kim. It would be insulting to say she is a natural domestic, because being a domestic is so looked-down upon. Kim and I have discussed this, and we agree there is a difference between service and being a servant. Serve, service, servile, servant. It's a spectrum. Love at one end, degradation at the other. One is clean enough to pass, but the other shimmers.

In early May a friendly couple came to the after-Mass get-together to shake everyone's hand and tell us they, too, were opening a business in Moratinos – another pilgrim accommodation.

Pilar had sold her family's prime slice of threshing floor to Roberto and Gerda, a rather oddly matched Spanish-German couple. Builders were there that very moment, marking out perimeters with strings on the flat lawn right where the Camino comes into town. It would not be a hotel, they said, but a small, two-star hostel. They would market online, charge a cool 30 Euros for a single, and skim off the upper end of the pilgrim market.

Roberto had walked the Way, and was keen to cash-in on the growing flow of well-heeled tourist pilgrims. There was no other lodging of this kind in the area. It would fill a market niche, he said. Gerda, a jolly German lady, promised organic vegetarian food, geothermal heating, and "bio" everything. The blueprints showed two stories of rendered concrete block, not adobe. The building was not exactly harmonious with the town around it, but it would not clash. It was not too tall, or brassy, or ugly.

At least it's not a *puticlub*, Juan said. Not a whorehouse.

And so the Holy Year brought change to our little town – a new Italian pilgrim albergue underway on the main street, smart new hostel going in at the other end of town.

The same week, over on the ridge above the Promised Land, the big wind-power turbines erected the summer before finally started turning.

15

FRED AND MAX

The first guitar concert happened in May, in the little Renaissance church of San Nicolas del Real Camino, the village next to ours. Rene Izquierdo and Elina Chekan, classical guitarists from Cuba and Belarus, played Bach and Mangore. The audience was small, but the sun shone through the high windows and illuminated the golden retablo while the notes bounced beautifully off the old stones. We chose San Nicolas over Moratinos because there were pilgrims at the albergue over there, and the concerts were meant for pilgrims. Besides, the church in St. Nicolas is prettier than ours.

It was a humble start, but a good one.

Fred, a seasonal Moratinos phenomenon, was over the moon. That little debut was the start of his dream coming true.

Fred was born in Mexico and raised in Pittsburgh, and in winter he lives in Wisconsin. In summer he comes over to Spain. Fred is, depending on which day it is, a chiropractor, an osteopathic doctor, sports medicine provider to the Green Bay Packers football team and/or U.S. Olympic bicycle team, and professional expert witness in medical malpractice trials.

He's pedaled a bike around the world and been flattened twice by drunk drivers. He's run with the bulls in Pamplona, explored the Amazon jungle, and schmoozed with lords and ladies. But most of all, Fred is a luthier. He builds concert-quality classical guitars.

His camino story goes thus: One fine day many years ago, as he hiked the Camino de Santiago, Fred sat down exhausted and realized he hadn't heard any music for days. He swore a great swear to St. James that someday he'd bring guitarists to that god-forsaken stretch of the Camino, to present great live music to the poor pilgrims. (The pilgrims' willingness to sit through 45 minutes of classical music after walking 30 kilometers was not part of the equation.)

Fred may be a lunatic, but he keeps his promises. The god-forsaken place where he made his vow was just east of here.

Late in April, Fred came to Moratinos with a handmade guitar for our house and a great big idea: A concert series through the summer, in emblematic churches here in Palencia province. He'd bring in his friends and clients and their students as featured artists, the diocese could provide an old rectory where they could stay, and the pilgrims and locals could enjoy a bit of culture in the evenings. Artists could beef up their resumes and soak up some Spanish ambience. We of

The Peaceable could be pioneers, co-founders of the non-profit cultural association that would back the whole thing.

We'd dealt for years with diabolical Spanish bureaucrats, but a Spanish Catholic Diocese looked like an even deeper ring of Hell. Fred's prospects did not fill us with hope.

We already had a lot going on, and guitars do not figure big in our lives. Driving guitarists around the country somehow did not appeal. Still, I introduced Fred to the few important people I knew. His Spanish was appalling, but his enthusiasm was infectious. He charmed the nuns in Carrion de los Condes, the priests in Fromista, the diocesan canon in charge of arts programs. On a feast day, when the city was on lockdown, the dotty old priest opened up the Bishop's Palace and showed us the art treasures stashed inside. He unlocked the glass cases in the treasury so we could hold in our hands the golden patens and jeweled monstrances. Father Calvo unlocked the treasury. Fred unlocked the diocese.

Fred set to work on us, too. He put new wiper blades on the car, repaired the plumbing in the little kitchen, and installed an irrigation system in the garden beds out back. He and Patrick spent hours in Sahagun at the Bar Deportivo, watching bullfights on the big-screen TV. Una liked Fred, and Tim was besotted with him.

One wine-soaked afternoon I found Fred in the cool,

dark barn, snoring softly on the sofa, draped in dogs.

Fred was fifty-something, with a Michelin spread and wild eyes and curly, wild white hair. He is loud and silly and very American, but somehow he's got something going on. Otherwise-sane and responsible people sign on to his schemes. They support them with their time and work and money.

And this scheme, the first of many to come, was the best.

There's something about live music, the first couple of moments when the sound fills the space and vibrates there like a living thing. The notes vanish within moments, but I believe live music stays inside a building, even after it passes from our ears. It settles like dust on the plaster, it curls itself into the swirls carved into the columns. It joins the architecture of the place where it's played. An old church or concert hall has centuries of music embedded in its domes and pews and moldings. And when a singer sings, or a guitarist or organist or choir opens up and pours out a new tune, it shakes loose the thousands of Psalms that were sung there, the million Masses chanted, drums and horns and clarinets from all the festivals and weddings, accordions and shepherds' flutes and birdsong, and all the clanging bells in the tower above. For a few moments of almost any concert I can hear a little extra layer of sound. It is the music peculiar to that place, shaking down from the rafters.

That sunny evening in St. Nicolas, the virgins smiled wide in their niches as Rene and Elina, two masters, pulled 500 years of ghosts out of the walls.

Word spread fast. Fred got his approvals, and we went ahead and wrote up a series of concerts – mostly for over east, where noble churches loom over towns with plenty of pilgrim traffic. We made sure Moratinos got one concert per month, alongside a Sunday Mass, when the greatest number of people could come and hear.

Kim made a video out in the corral. Rene played a fancy flamenco tune outside the chicken run, while Una Dog relaxed on the ground at his feet. He finished with a flourish, the sun flashed off the face of the guitar, and as if on cue, Max the Rooster crowed a lovely crow.

I am not a great fan of classical guitar music, but that is what landed here, and it's what we've got. "High culture" doesn't happen much in Moratinos. The locals were suspicious at first, and grew bored when the Bach partitas went wheezing on for too long. Still, they knew we meant well. They showed up, most of them, when the concert Sunday came around. They took their medicine, and sometimes they liked it. Angela, a friend to all foreign visitors, was a program stalwart. She wore her best dresses, and often announced the performers in both English and Spanish.

Outside, the fields waved with grain. Pilgrims lightened up our days, and we all spent much more time out in the sunshine. The greyhounds hid away in the barn when strangers came, but they slowly learned it was safe to say hello, and that pilgrims sometimes carry sausages. Una was a master of the chin-on-the-knee charm. Tim, with his velvet fur and puppy-dog eyes, always snuggled up to the visitors who most missed their own dogs. He did not mind them stroking him for hours. He knew it was good for them.

Nabi and Lulu watched from the barn door. The galgo girls saw Tim and Una enjoying human company. They wanted to, too.

Out in the open, free in the fields, the galgos were transformed. They were grace embodied, slender and fast, breathtakingly beautiful. Out there, they didn't mind us touching them. They scooped up our hands with their pointy noses, asking for scratches. Occasionally they'd flush out a quail or rabbit or hare, and we'd see just what they were bred for.

It was inconceivable that hunters had thrown them away. These dogs were splendid hunters, far as we could tell – but we are not hunters ourselves. Perhaps their terrible fearfulness made them no good at sports. Maybe they were gun-shy, or inbred, not up to the breed standard. Or maybe they'd just gotten separated from their handlers. They certainly were not intelligent dogs, but they were beauties. Portly Tim enjoyed prancing down the trail with a galgo on each side, like Elton John walking the red carpet with a couple of supermodels.

Out in the back garden, magnificent Max the cockerel ruled supreme over his seven hens, but all was not happiness. Max was turning mean. Three of the girls had chunks of feathers missing from their necks and backs. They were bloody from Max gouging them with his spurs and beak when he mounted them. We went into the pen a couple of times each day to feed and water the chickens and collect the eggs, and we soon began bringing along a stick. Max didn't like visitors.

He especially hated Patrick. A male, no doubt a rival for the hens' affections. When Patrick busied himself with the feed barrel, Max made running leaps at him, wings flapping and spurs flying. It wasn't really dangerous, but it was plenty intimidating, especially if you wore short pants. And it was boring, especially when we needed to do maintenance in there. Just try pitching and stacking straw-bales with a Tasmanian Devil thrashing away at your pantlegs.

I grew up with chickens, so I knew what to do. I gave Max a good crack with a broomstick early on, and he left me alone. Paddy was another story. One morning at feeding time, Patrick had enough of all the beak and claws. Max jumped up at him, and Patrick kicked him – caught him a clean blow right off the toe of his boot. Max flew backward, bounced off the wire fence and hit the ground hard. A moment passed, he didn't move, Patrick wondered if the old boy was finished.

But Max opened his eyes, picked himself up, shook his feathers back into place, and came blasting right back for more. I heard them out there, Patrick laughing and shouting at the same time, swearing at that damn rooster.

16

BELIEVERS

The garden beds sprouted radishes, carrots, and peas, the rows all wavy from Murphy Cat using it for a litter-box. Kim went to hike with her mystical boyfriend, a prison guard from Mannheim. Fred went off to buy exotic wood in Belgium.

It was wonderful being at home, walking up the tractor trails on Sunday morning with the happy dogs running alongside, the bells calling over the fields to summon us all to church.

Not everybody went to Mass on Sunday, but it was a good idea to be there.

Belief is optional. Long wintertime conversations showed me I was one of very few people in town who has an interest in things theological. Everyone had the prayers and responses dinned into them from childhood, and everyone recited them, letter-perfect and at a good volume, at the proper moments. Even Fran, whose grip on reality was fragile, zipped along through the Nicene Creed a half-beat ahead of everyone else. Everyone sits in the same pew, with the same people each Sunday, not necessarily family.

The pews are handmade from cheap pine. They wobble on the uneven floor. They are spectacularly uncomfortable, but Mass rarely takes longer than 30 minutes. With all the standing and kneeling figured-in, suffering is minimal.

The Camino guides say the building is "of no artistic merit." No one can say how old it is, and someone told us a wicked priest at some point sold-off the retablo and all the statues of any value. What he left us is a mishmash of simpering plaster saints and a stripped-bare sanctuary with surprisingly fine acoustics.

It is a little church, humble. We're not many people, but our location on the Camino de Santiago won us some special consideration. We still had a Mass every Sunday, presented by Don Santiago, a small, smiling, snowy-haired man who was supposed to be retired.

Moratinos stands out from other congregations because we sing. We sing the consecration song and the "Alleluias" before the Gospel reading, and when we march a statue around the town in procession we sing an odd assortment of chirpy choruses and lugubrious dirges. We sing very loud and very badly, but no one cares. It is fun, it is healthy. And where else, when else, do we all get to sing together?

Still, at the climax of the weekly rite, almost nobody takes Communion. Of the 15 or so people who attend on an average

Sunday, only three or four of us regularly go up to have our little bit of Jesus.

I used to wonder if I should go to Communion, if I was being self-righteous, but any time I skipped I had to answer to Remedios. Three is the minimum number permitted, she said. If the number of communicants fell below that, the bishop would suspend our weekly Masses and Moratinos would just dry up.

Later on I realized how much I needed that Communion. It's spiritual food. My lifestyle could be a real drain on the spirits. I have to keep my strength up.

Maybe that's why those of us who consistently took the sacrament were women. Maybe we didn't have so many opportunities to sin during the week. Or maybe, as the ones taking care of everybody else, we needed that little bit of community-sanctioned self-care. I don't like to go without it. Whenever I miss out on Sunday Mass, I feel oddly wrong, like I didn't take my vitamin, or I didn't call my mom.

The church bells sometimes pull pilgrims in from the trail. The devout among them leave their backpacks by the baptismal font and join us in the pews. Almost no one ever greets them.

But me, the cheerful post-evangelical, I do. Some Sundays in summer, when the plaza was full of pilgrims, I go out before the service and invite people to come in and join us.

Pilgrims complain bitterly at the number of churches along the pathway that are locked up, but when the opportunity comes to join in a parish Mass, they can't say "No" quick enough. "I'm a pilgrim," they say. "I don't have time for church. I have to walk."

It makes me smile, but I feel a little rejected, too. What the hell kind of pilgrim won't go to church? They want to see inside the building. They want a museum of art or ethnography, something safely under glass. But if you offer them the living Christ, and pews full of sinners? No thanks, man. This is my camino, done on my terms.

Time was, not so long ago, that only one or two pilgrims ever passed through this town in a given year. They were treated with respect and a bit of awe, and were almost always seminarians, monks, or priests. They were always religious, always men. Proper women stayed at home, and men not linked to the church didn't wander the countryside unless they were up to no good, or atoning for some great sin.

If a pilgrim appeared he'd often be asked inside to share whatever the family had – garlic soup, stewed lentils or garbanzos, an apple, a chunk of bread and sheep's milk cheese, a porron of wine. The traveler blessed the household, then took himself off to the church porch or the threshing floor to sleep. If he was lucky he could bed down in the barn, or sleep in the bunkhouse with the hired men. There was never any question of him paying for his stay. Hosting a pilgrim was not a transaction.

In Sahagun, right up through the 1960's, pilgrims slept in the town hall. There was a little room set aside for them, with a sleeping niche carved into the adobes. The straw bedding was changed once a year. A Belgian pilgrim who stayed there in the 1950s said it was hopping with fleas.

Pilgrims were penitents, professional sufferers. If there was a holy service anywhere, they'd be sure to attend, be they baptisms, funerals, weddings, or fiestas – having a pilgrim show up was a lucky sign, and the traveler often was invited home to share in the feast that followed.

Pilgrims were dirty and hungry, homeless by choice, but they played a role in villages all over Spain. They gave the locals a way to put the Gospel into action, to feed the hungry and welcome the stranger without taking on the risks that come with gypsies or transients. The family that took in pilgrims was publicly acknowledged as doing a Christian deed, and the pilgrim, conveniently, moved right along the following day. It was easier to be nice to pilgrims than, say, the neighbors. Or even family.

Big towns like Sahagun or Carrion de los Condes long

ago had big pilgrim hostels, run by pious confraternities or monastic houses. But by the 20th century, wars and enlightenment and the general suspicion that goes with dictatorship put an end to pilgrimages. The Camino de Santiago was dead, but for a few academics and fanatics.

Generalissimo Franco saw himself as a conquering hero in the mold of St. James, but his Camino was the N-120 highway. Church groups took buses and trains to Santiago for annual patriotic fiestas, but walking the Camino was just a memory in Spain. Large sections of the old pilgrim road were paved- or plowed-over. Pilgrim inns fell to ruin, or were converted to hay barns or bunkhouses for itinerant workers.

No one can say just why the Camino de Santiago came blazing back to life in the last three decades. The death of Franco, a drive for athletic challenges, spiritual thirst, capitalism, nostalgia, historic memory... some, or all the above, have part in it.

Little clutches of history students no longer roll out their sleeping bags on the floor of the abandoned school-house. Gone are the grubby holy men, sleeping rough on the threshing floor, begging crusts from the farmers, praying their Rosaries as they walk.

Now the pilgrims come by the tens of thousands, and they're met on arrival by travel agents, restaurateurs, guide-book publishers, tourist boards, and "personal-growth coaches."

The dirty old schoolhouse is transformed to one of almost 500 inns, B&Bs, albergues, hostels, or other places geared to pilgrims, scattered along the main Camino pathways. Pilgrims are consumers now, with an array of choices on where to stay and how much to spend. They have books to tell them the history of each town along the road, the art treasures hidden inside the locked-up churches, (and who has the keys), local cuisine specialties, all the Must-See Attractions of each day of their 30-day program.

For the more spiritually minded there are prayer books and spirit guides to ensure they don't miss a single Sacred Space on their Inner Journey. Others keep tabs on the "Best Value for Money" options, so their pilgrimage doesn't start costing like a vacation. Some pilgrims are ever vigilant about their money and time. They are here for a short time, and they are spending money, too. Pilgrims like to believe the locals would still be living in Stone-Age huts if it weren't for them and their cash.

What was a rugged path of repentance and suffering is now a series of day-hikes for spiritual consumers. The bare-bones infrastructure for ascetics has become a cheap holiday attraction for those whose eyes glitter at "something for nothing." The historic Pilgrim Way is a collision of Capitalism and old-time Christian simplicity. The outcomes are fascinating, moving, and sometimes grotesque.

We live in the middle of it.

For some people, walking the Camino has become an addiction. They return year after year, they walk over and over. Their trail diaries comprise a whole genre of Camino lore of wildly varying quality. Hobos live on the Camino, or live off it, traveling from one "free" albergue to the next, begging for their bed and board. Trail life is cheaper than daily life in many European cities, so laid-off workers just hang out on the Camino, killing time until they can go home and collect their pensions.

Bearded men wander the trail, costumed in the brown robes and broad hats of 16th century pilgrims. They eat and drink for free at cafes, and sell signed photos of themselves staring off into the distance in a tragically holy way.

Creative, enterprising souls become "Camino Coaches," they ease the way for less-confident pilgrims and thus subsidize their own wandering habits. Others create Camino-themed jewelry, ribbons, sunscreen, fortune-telling cards, hiking poles, water bottles, hats, socks, and stickers, and sell them on the internet as well as at souvenir stands and albergues along the Way. There are Camino trade shows, conferences, campaigns, and clubs.

Not all these things are bad. Camino Amigos groups run several albergues where pilgrims can sleep for a donation, to keep the trail open for truly poor pilgrims. Sadly, the facilities are often worn-out and neglected, overrun by middle-class tourists gleefully sleeping for free, soaking up the grubby "Real Camino" ambience.

There still are real pilgrims out there. Many of them start out as tourists, but find their thoughts turning to deeper, wider things as they walk. No matter how pimped and paved the path becomes, it is still very long, hard, and sometimes lonely. It is an old, holy place, made sacred by the footsteps of millions of people, over a thousand years.

17

NIGHT SKY

Castilians are practical people. They leave the witches and evil-eyes and fortune-telling to the Basques and Gallegos and gypsies. They go to church on Sunday, and get on with their lives. They are remarkably free of curiosity.

One balmy, clear evening I was out along the N-120 right at sundown with my new telescope, trying in the failing light to get it lined-up to magnetic north. I was only just learning to use the thing, getting my head around the concepts of sky maps and deep-space objects and celestial navigation. It was tough going, but I made progress.

Ever since an eighth-grade course in Earth and Space Science, I'd wanted to know what astronomy was all about. I signed up for Astronomy 101 at university, but the only stars I got to know were members of the football squad. It turned out to be a "gut class," an easy science credit for athletes and other less-than gifted students. I attended fewer than half the class sessions, took the exams, and scored an A.

One of the pleasures of early retirement is grabbing back these lost opportunities. I bought myself a stubby cylinder telescope, and read up on how to use it. I set it up out back on dark nights, coated myself in mosquito repellant, and had some breathtaking sessions of star-gazing. Moratinos is at 900 meters altitude, and there's precious little light or air pollution hanging between the telescope and heaven.

Antonio Machado, a writer with a penchant for these plains, said "the scenery of Castile is in the skies." The clouds in the daytime are spectacular, but he must've also gone out after sundown. Things are visible in those deep, clear depths that cannot be seen from any other place I've been.

I can't say exactly what I saw at first, that balmy evening. I used a little flashlight to carefully calibrate my tripod and compass and planisphere map, then shut off the light and let my eyes adjust. I aimed for quasars, black holes, slowly blinking Cephiad variables. Often as not, I saw only tiny points of light that could've been anything. For consolation I'd end up looking at whatever planets were visible: good old bright Venus and Mercury, shiny pink Mars. Or just the moon.

I will never forget the adrenaline thrill the first time I closed-in on Saturn, and saw those wonderful rings – it was like seeing the Grand Canyon for the first time, after a lifetime of photos and TV images. It was for real! Somehow, once I spent twenty minutes peering at it through my telescope, it became mine. Even if it was 20 times the size of earth, or 750 million miles away, it was part of me. One of my planets, one my friends, mine to view.

At least until the hulking form of Modesto hove into the viewfinder. He startled the hell out of me. "What are you doing out here in the dark?" he chuckled, shining his police-grade flashlight on me.

"Am I under arrest?" I asked. I squelched my peevishness, squeezed shut my eyes to preserve the openness of my pupils.

Modesto was well into his 80s. He didn't usually come out after dark. He must've been intrigued indeed to come out along the highway so late at night, clear up on the other end of the village.

Modesto is a considerable intellect. He spent his life plowing and reaping, but he read, too, all those years, and he wrote. Modesto is a writer. His "Memories of a Laborer" memoir sold out its first two printings, and gave us an impressive primer on Moratinos life when we first arrived. Modesto may not be highly educated, but he's smart. It wouldn't do to underestimate him.

"I am looking at M81, a bright spiral galaxy," I told him. "Or I'm trying to. It's supposed to be more visible now than ever before. The smeary thing right up there in the handle on the Big Dipper. The Plough."

Modesto pointed his flashlight at the sky and squinted after it. "We call that the wagon," he said. "There's a galaxy in there that you can see?"

"You can barely see it with just your eyes, but yes, it is there tonight," I said. "If you have a telescope, and you're pointing it just right, it's supposed to be *una maravilla.* I'm not sure I have it yet. I am not even sure I will know when I do have it. I am still just learning," I said. "I don't have a teacher. I just have books, and the internet."

"Well, then. Let's have a look," Modesto said. He handed me his light. I switched it off. I shouldn't have. He moved round behind the telescope, where the eyepiece pointed upward. I tried to show him where to put his eye, how to position himself. His knee bumped the tripod. His hand bumped the eyepiece. Jesus, I thought, I will never find anything out there, ever again!

"Here," I said. "Put your hand here, your eye here." Our foreheads collided, I saw a big flash of light that wasn't really there.

Modesto stood quietly, peering into the eyepiece. He inhaled, clicked his dentures, moved his glasses off his eyes, and looked again.

"Rebekah," he said quietly. "Look at this. Just look."

He stood away. I looked. I didn't expect to see anything.

"What do you think that is?" I asked him.

"Is that your galaxy?"

I peered really hard. There were two stars in the viewer. I slowly turned the big knob. I turned the little knob. And yes, it really was there. It really was.

"Modesto," I whispered. "Modesto, you're right. Look!"

He looked. He inhaled. He put his glasses on and looked again.

"That's it. That's the M81!" I said. "See the spiral?"

"Hostia!" he swore. "That thing is another world? It looks like a fried egg!"

"It's a whole other galaxy of other worlds."

"No mi digas," he said. "You don't say."

He stood up. He pulled off his glasses and wiped them with his shirttail. He bowed again and peered into the eyepiece. "You're sure?"

"Yes," I said. I was not totally sure, but who was checking? "That's the one."

"I shall have to tell Raquel," he said. "I will put it in my blog. You shall have to write that down for me. The name of the galaxy, I mean. Which galaxy it is."

"Of course," I said. I put my eye back down, just to reassure myself. Somehow, with his knees and elbows, Modesto had found what 10 minutes of my fiddling with instruments could not. I looked at the smear of stars in the viewfinder, and a bubble of laughter rose in my throat. Joy. It was joy, to see something so far away, to bring it so near, to feel so small and at the same moment like I'd seen an angel.

And I had a witness. I had someone to share it with, an 80-something Castilian farmer, a fellow soul with a streak of curiosity. We clapped one another on the back and laughed out loud. I thanked him. He thanked me. He shook my hand.

He took his *linterna* and lit his way back home, smiling the smile of an explorer, someone who's seen something great for the very first time, out in the back yard.

18

PENTECOST

The church year wound round to the Feast of Pentecost, a sign that the harvest is coming, if not the Holy Spirit.

The sun shone bright, the birds sang out, the priest wore his scarlet robes. On the way home I stopped over at Angela's house to say hello, to cuddle the new kittens, to see if she wanted to hike that afternoon. Angela didn't go to church, except for big holidays or baptisms. The church had evolved too far away from the simple carpenter who founded it, she told me. She couldn't relate to it.

That's what we talked about, out walking on Sundays: honesty and hypocrisy, men and women, love and romance. Her family was tight-knit, ruled-over by Pablo, her much loved, arch-conservative dad. Angela had a gift for children, for teaching and travel. Angela loved English, too, but she didn't want to teach English forever. She wanted to live English, and teach whatever else. In English.

It wasn't going to be easy, starting from where she was, but she was still young, she still had time. And she had a good job now, with students who wanted to learn. In Salas she had a position she could get her teeth into.

One red-letter day the previous autumn I'd gone to Angela's school and spoke to the English classes with my American accent. The kids thought I was a scream, a character right out of The Simpsons, unbelievable. They wanted to sit next to me, and hold my hands. They wanted a photo with me and Miss Angela. They wanted my autograph!

Angela and I spent a couple of weekends driving around Burgos province, seeing the sights. She drove us over the mountains into Soria one bright October Saturday. We picked mushrooms from the leaf litter on a steep, wooded hillside, and browsed a busy Fungus Fair in a school gym. An expert said our finds were niscalos, chanterelles, and boletus, all of them delicious and perfectly safe to eat. Angela had the restaurant next door fry them up for us. I was terribly allergic to the mushrooms. Angela wouldn't even taste them. But she spent a whole day doing mushroom things, because I was interested.

Likewise, she showed me spooky Visigothic burial sites, stone tombs cut into rocks, crude churches and hermit caves carved out of remote hillsides. She tolerated my churchy ways, sitting through lugubrious Gregorian Vespers sung by the Benedictines at Silos. She took me to church at Salas de los Infantes, where the heads of seven murdered princes are kept in medieval silver boxes behind the altar. Angela didn't know the legend of the heads, whose they were and how they got there. It never occurred to her to ask. She was not curious, but she indulged my curiosity.

That's how she was, and I loved her. Paddy and I called on her when Spanish vocabulary or bureaucracy proved too much, and she smoothed the way. She was a standby. The Peaceable couldn't have happened without her.

And I was her friend, too.

"Get your shoes on, Angela!" I sang out as I came through the door that Pentecost Sunday morning. "The weather is lovely, it's time to walk!" Angela held open the door for me. In true Pentecostal fashion, a sparrow came in, too. It flew over our heads and through the hall and into the sun porch out back, where it slammed itself senseless against the glass. Angela called for her mother to bring a pot with a lid, to capture it, get it outside. I felt a little flutter of superstitious fear. A bird inside the house, oh no! Bad luck!

I snatched up the bird in a tea-towel. It was very much alive. "It's Pentecost," I said, smiling. "Here is our dove of peace!" I opened the back door into the patio and pitched the bird outside. It fluttered to the concrete.

"Thank you, Rebekah!" Angela sang out, hunkered over,

tying her shoes. She didn't see, but I did. A barn cat snatched up the luckless bird and sloped off to the barn.

It's a good thing I am not superstitious, I thought. That would've been a bad sign.

19

HOUSEHOLD SAINTS

That was a spectacular summer, with a parade of pilgrims and visitors. Tim Dog wandered away and was lost in the woods near Ledigos, miles from home. Hours later he arrived on the doorstep. He found his way home on his own. Una dog spent afternoons over at the albergue project, keeping Bruno company.

The Lord Jesus came and stayed with us. Rainer, a German pilgrim, assured us he is this generation's embodiment of Jesus Christ. Rainer refused to take showers. He would only immerse himself, which required a bathtub. There are not very many bathtubs in the albergues on The Way. We gave thanks to God that we had one. I think his fellow pilgrims were thankful, too. His laundry could almost rise up and walk.

At dinnertime Rainer blessed the bread and wine and broke the loaf and passed around bits to everyone, but after that he slipped back to almost normal. He unloaded just a bit on Patrick, whom he'd met before when he passed our way. After 30 years of marriage, his wife had left him, Rainer said. "I don't understand how she could do that, after all this time," he sighed.

Patrick is always the soul of compassion. "Imagine, living for 30 years with Jesus Christ," he said. "I'm amazed she stayed more than thirty minutes."

Rainer was courageous, he didn't mind being laughed-at. He blessed us all when he left, and I thanked him for it. You never know which of these people is an angel, and which is just a guy. Far as I know, Rainer is the only Incarnate Christ to stay with us. Unless you count the Christ that lives in everyone, and everything.

Soon after, a professor of Sacred Geology stayed with us, a teacher at Naropa Institute in Colorado, a real New-Ager. She traveled with dousing rods, and could tell by how they twisted in her hands where water flowed below our feet in underground streams, or where telluric energy flowed through the rocks. Our salon, where the pilgrims sleep, is a spot of great quiet and peace, she said. Out in the back garden her dousing rods bobbed above the same old well and vein of fresh water that an engineering firm had found, back when we'd pondered installing a geothermal heating system.

Sonomi stayed, too. Sonomi was a Japanese pilgrim who trained in Canada to be a hospitalera. She was tiny and shy, and was overwhelmed by her first assignment – the gigantic "pilgrim factory" albergue in Ponferrada. I went and fetched her away. We told her it's OK, not everyone is cut out for hosting pilgrims. She sat quietly and watched how we do things at the Peaceable. She got bored, I think. After a couple of days she took the train back to Ponferrada and her post there, and finished it out like a champ.

I rescued another hospitalera that summer from a little albergue in a remote Galician village. Her fellow host was abusive, she said – insulting, arrogant, bossy. I'd suffered a similar fate myself the year before, at that same albergue, so I went and fetched her away, too. The rescuee turned out to be suffering all kinds of family trauma back home in Ontario. Spending her holidays caring for strangers wasn't a great idea just then.

She was a character. She looked into my past lives one afternoon, and discovered why I am so deeply attached to this place. It seems I once was a monk, brought up in a local village and educated at the great Benedictine monastery that once reigned over Sahagun. Having lived and died in the neighborhood 600 years ago, it was no wonder I was drawn back here again, she said.

What the hell. Why not? It would also explain why I like going to church.

We had the rota of guitarists set to play through the

summer. I posted it on the church door like Martin Luther. For the Holy Year the diocese agreed to open all the Camino churches through the summer, to pay a nominal amount to each village to open up and hang around so the multitude of pilgrims could stop inside and pray. Don Santiago made up a schedule, starting in July, a day each week for each household. The hours were well outside the times when most pilgrims passed through town, but then the program was set up by people who'd never met a real pilgrim.

There's no arguing with priests, everyone agreed.

We took our day each week, sitting at a little desk in the entryway, greeting the passers-by, stamping pilgrim credentials with a Moratinos seal Patrick designed. We brought a little boom box down with us, and played Gregorian chants in the background.

The neighbors came in and sat in the cool shade. Little Gillen and Olaya came. We played Hangman, they coached me on past-tense verbs and laughed at the awful things I do to Spanish. They are brother and sister, they live in Vittoria, in Basque Country, and come to Moratinos in summer. They wandered the town with several cousins, watched-over by everyone.

We've watched them grow up. They study English at school, but speak Spanish at home, and Basque. There are several

Basque-speakers in town; Olaya and Gillens' great uncles left town years ago and found work in Vittoria and Bilbao, married Basque women, raised their kids with both languages. We are not the only Spanish-as-Second-Language speakers here.

Gillen and Olaya kept me company at the church. Late one morning Angela arrived, and pulled a newborn kitten from her handbag to show the children. It made an awful racket. It was almost closing time anyway, so I locked up the church with the two huge keys, and headed down to Angela's house to see the rest of the litter.

The babies were finger-sized, incredibly small, and wiggly. Their mother wasn't far past kittenhood herself. She'd made a nest in the straw in the tractor shed, beneath the tines of the hay rake. We all squeezed into the space, oohed and aahed over the catlings. Gillen counted and sorted the babies by color, then reattached them to their mother in proper order. A shaft of sunlight lit up the scene like a Caravaggio. I could feel the sharp tines of the rake just overhead, way too near our eyes and ears. I cringed a little.

No one else gave it any thought. Farmers waste so little time on fear.

Sunflowers bloom in July, great wide fields of smiling yellow faces. Patrick says they are vulgar and gaudy. They bloom just in time for our wedding anniversary, so we always have a million reminders. July is my favorite month, the peak of the year. The night sky is full of falling stars, villages throw parties to celebrate their patron saints. That year, pilgrims came and came and came.

Amado came, a Redemptorist priest from the Philippines. He was small and wiry and very holy, he walked barefoot, for peace. He stayed up late with me and sat quietly meditating, 40 minutes without a word. No other pilgrim ever did that.

I went to one of Fred's guitar concerts in Fromista one evening, and brought home two young nuns. Their grey habits were wrinkled and spotted, and one of them had a terrible cold. They spoke some English, so we managed well. They were French, from a relatively new contemplative order that was falling on hard times. Of the twenty sisters who lived there, they were the youngest and most fit. They were chosen to make the pilgrimage to Santiago for the sake of the entire convent.

They had almost no money. Until they started walking, neither of them had been outside the convent walls for the previous eight years. They'd set out from their front gate, expecting to find accommodations at the nunneries and churches along the Way. They quickly learned different.

"We stop at the convent, introduce ourselves, tell them

we're pilgrims. The sisters are always happy to see us," Sor Miryam said. "They sit us down, they give us cakes and tea. They show us the empty beds in the novitiate wing and ask us to pray for them, because they have no younger sisters joining. But when we ask if we can stay with them that night, they say No, hospitality is not part of the ministry of their order. They send us to the pilgrim albergue."

"We feel like Our Lady and Saint Joseph, no room at the inn!" said Sor Ana.

"Or maybe the Holy Family, on the way to Egypt. We had one woman at Mass in Najera invite us to stay at her house, but when we arrived her husband closed the door in our faces. It was dark already."

"We'd given up our beds at the albergue."

"That place was full of young men. Bicyclists. They wear the most extraordinary outfits," Ana said. "We felt... we felt like maybe we shouldn't sleep there, with them. They'd been drinking. We slept outside."

"We slept in a vineyard. It was all we could do, at the end."

"We did not make such a good choice."

"I think that is when I caught the cold."

They stayed three days. We asked them to bless our dinner, and they sang a beautiful little psalm. Tim loved them. Their laundry hung in strange shapes on the line, and they took one another's photos, wearing our African caftan robes while their habits dried. They were funny and bright, and good cooks, too.

It was hard to say goodbye.

The holiest people we met that summer weren't religious at all, but I called them the Trinity.

One was a 50-something woman from Slovakia, a teacher of languages. She spoke five or six fluently, and happily one was English. He name was Norma. Her skin was pale, her eyes were dark circles under bushy brows. She was unremarkable but for her companions.

Karsten and Eric were slender, young, and blonde, two 20-year-old youths from Germany, well-off and well-spoken. They were doing the Camino for sport, they said, to keep in shape over summer for their school-year athletic pursuits. They'd met Norma at a spring outside Burgos, where she was giving herself a vitamin injection. Eric, a keen vegetarian, had asked about her combination of nutrients.

The shots kept her going, she said. Norma was doing the Camino that summer because she was running out of time. Cancer in her lymph nodes had gone to her brain. Inoperable. But she still could walk just fine, she said. If she was going to make The Way, it was now or never. Karsten and Eric thought that was amazing. They walked with her to the next town, and checked in at the pilgrim shelter.

Someone told the manager that evening that Norma was in the dormitory shooting-up heroin. The hospitalero threw her out. Karsten and Eric shouted out her defense, but the man wouldn't hear it. So they gathered up their things and left, too.

The three of them spent the night on the church porch, and walked together from then on. The boys took turns walking ahead and behind. They didn't hover, but they kept Norma in sight. They scouted water fountains, and good places to stay. That's how they came to the Peaceable, Karsten said. He'd read about us in his Paderborn Pilgrim Guide.

We don't list ourselves in guides, but the guy who makes up the Paderborn Guide is a friend. This is how it works.

That's how it worked, for Norma. "my blue-eyed angels," she called the boys. "Sent from heaven."

That's how it worked for Eric. "This would've been another achievement, a nice long-distance hike, some beers, maybe a girlfriend. But with Norma, we have meaning. She tells us many things we never heard of. We help her. We have purpose."

In an antiques shop I found a little image of St. James, 18th century, from France, carved from pear wood by some amateur whittler. It was just a little cartoony, just right for our church. I bought it. I asked Segundino the carpenter to make a wall plinth for him, so we could put him up front where the pilgrims could see him. We have a fine statue of San Roque, a pilgrim saint, proof against plagues – he even has a miracle story attached. But what's a church along the Santiago trail without a Santiago inside?

No one could find a reason why not. Maribel arranged to have him blessed and installed in August, part of the town fiesta Mass. Segundino set to work.

On our next day of church duty I climbed up a ladder and plucked the silver crown off the Virgin Mary's head. I took a soft cloth and some polish and worked it over, rubbing hard to remove the tarnish of many years. I found the crown wasn't silver at all – just some soft pot metal, molded and soldered and battered-about. Still, someone had put their heart and their savings into it, perhaps a thank-you for an answered prayer. Had it been silver, the wicked priest would've sold that, too.

Like a lot of Spanish virgin statues, this one has a spike growing out of her head, installed for just such a crown. But even with jewels, this Blessed Mother is a plain country girl. Her smile is a little too wide, her eyes too close together. She's not a Holy Queen of Heaven. She's one of us.

20

FIESTA

Summer stretched out. The farmers cut the grain, baled and stacked the straw, then took a break. It was celebration time in Moratinos, the feast day of Santo Tomas Apostol, our doubting patron.

Fiesta weekend is a homecoming party for the families based in town, and cousins, aunts, and shirttail relations crowd in for the fun and food. Patrick and I have no family within 500 miles, but the fiesta still is an anniversary of sorts.

At the fiesta of 2006 we first found the farmhouse that became The Peaceable.

It's a long story, how we found the place, but we tell it over and over, because almost everyone who stays here wants to know: Why this town? How'd you get here?

We were volunteer hospitaleros. We'd looked around Spain and served at albergues all over the several Caminos that lead to Santiago. We had some idea of where we might like to settle, so we volunteered that summer in towns we knew we liked already: Fuenterroble de Salvatierra, and Hervas, down on the Via de la Plata. Miraz, up on the Camino del Norte.

Ourense, just south of Santiago itself. We were on our way to volunteer in a little town near Burgos when we found Moratinos.

We stopped to say hello to a British couple who'd bought an old house there, who wanted to start an albergue of their own. We'd exchanged e-mails, they invited us to stop, they were jolly and merry and welcoming, every bit as enthusiastic as we were. The house with a blue door, they said. Come about noon. We drove from Salamanca on the hottest day of the year, pulled up five minutes early, and found the only house behind a blue door was a ruin. It was mud bricks and dust, hopping with field mice. No one was home. It looked like no one had been home for decades.

The couple were gone, we learned, off in Santiago to have a baby. "Feel free to stay," they texted back. "There's a yurt in the back garden."

We stayed three days, as long as we could stand it. There was a camp toilet and an electrical outlet, an extension line slung over a wall from a neighbors' house. We gave the passing pilgrims tea and coffee from the stores inside the ruin, served in elegant Japanese teapots and porcelain cups.

It was friendly and fun and kind of filthy. The yurt was airless but charming, a bit of Mongolia on the high plains of Spain.

But best of all were the people in that town.

We'd been warned about Castilians, that they're closed-off, cold and distrustful. But the people in Moratinos were warm. First to greet us was Fran, a man who's not all there. He shook our hands and sang us a song:

"The four cardinal compass points are something every Spaniard knows."

We met Toby, a squat, nervous, yappy dog. Soon after came Maribel, Fran's sister and caretaker. She said the ruin once belonged to her mother.

Remedios and Arturo owned the house next door, where the power cord was plugged-in.

Remedios' mother Vitoriana lived in the corner house on the plaza. Toby Dog lived at Remedios' house with her and Arturo and their sons Carlos and Juan. They ran the big family farm, and repaired combine harvesters deep into the night in a farmyard adjacent to the yurt.

They all made us welcome. In the cool of the evening the town sat in plastic chairs outside Vitoriana's house, playing complicated card games and trading gossip magazines. They sat us down and asked us where we were from, what we were doing there. They gave me Coca-Cola, because I am American. They gave Patrick beer, because he was a man, and it was summer.

They were glad to have us helping out with the pilgrims, because all of them had other work to do. There were an awful lot of pilgrims passing through, and they were bothersome sometimes, knocking on the doors, asking for food or toilets or directions, or the keys to the church.

Patrick and I liked Moratinos. It wasn't historic or pretty, or even appealing, but it was dead-center on the Camino Frances, the major pilgrim route. Here was a town that needed help with pilgrims, and an albergue-to-be that obviously would need a hand in the future. We asked if any of the empty houses in town was for rent. Everyone laughed. They laughed when we said we liked the town, and that we liked them.

They said no one comes here to stay, that the town was on its way out. But if we liked it so well, we should come back in August to the fiesta, and see it when it's most alive, when all the empty houses were full.

And that's what we did. We went back that August for the fiesta. The British still had not had their baby, they hadn't returned. We stayed in the yurt again, and danced in the plaza, and after lunch on Sunday we were invited to go and look at a derelict farmhouse on the edge of town. It was for sale.

It was during that night, after the Mobile Disco shut down,

I stepped out of the yurt and into the wee-hours silence and heard a hundred swallows whirring round the church tower. I looked up into the most spectacular field of stars I'd ever seen. Just then, a night bird sang out a perfect song.

That's when I knew. This was the home I'd looked for all my life.

Two fiestas later, we hung up the "Peaceable Kingdom" plaque and opened up our house on fiesta weekend to welcome all the neighbors in to see what we'd done to the place.

And this Holy Year, our fifth fiesta, guitarists from Camino Artes, the Freddy program, would play the "high-culture" concert in the church. Our little Santiago statue would take his place up front at the Iglesia de Santo Tomas. Segundino had bolted a triple-arched pear-wood perch onto the wall, and bolted Santi safely down, too. Remedios brought in two little vases with silk carnations to stand on either side. I put a beeswax candle by his elbow, and he was good to (never) go. Don Santiago duly sprinkled him during the big Mass. Santi himself looked a little embarrassed at all the fuss.

Remedios said he was the first new saint installed in a good thirty years. He makes her happy, she said, because a new saint gives a place a new lease on life. You don't see new saints in dying towns.

The procession and prayers and music went on, the rockets flared and boomed, the kiddies played bowls with a massive wooden ball and pins hand-carved who-knows-how-long-ago.

Out on the N120 two-lane, a French couple named Antoine and Amelie zipped eastward down the highway. Inside the backpacks in the trunk were two fresh Compostela certificates, dated the previous Thursday. They'd finished their pilgrimage, a trip they'd done over several years, one two-week chunk at a time. At dawn they'd held hands in a little church in Finisterre and sang a hymn. They climbed into their rental car and headed toward France and home.

On the road between San Nicolas and Moratinos their car veered off the road. It struck a culvert in the field and rolled over onto its roof. Antoine climbed out, woozy but unhurt. Amelie was trapped inside.

Fred was driving along the road behind them and saw the accident happen. He stopped, phoned the police, then scrambled down the bank and wriggled through the broken rear window of the crushed car. He couldn't un-do Amelie's safety belt, couldn't free her. He held her hand as she died.

Antoine was stunned, so Fred stayed with him. He put the man in his car and drove with him behind the ambulance to the hospital. He made sure Antoine was checked-over by a doctor. He took him to the morgue, and got him started on

the paperwork and decision-making. It was a holiday weekend in August. Nothing would happen until Monday. There
was nowhere for Antoine to go. So Fred brought him back to
Moratinos, to the Peaceable.

After the merry Mass we went home for lunch and found
Fred slumped in a kitchen chair with a glass of tinto in his
hand. There was blood on his clothes and skin and in his hair.
Antoine was upstairs in the green bedroom. Fred told us what
had happened.

We left Antoine alone for a while.

The man was numb and red-eyed, silent. He'd been on the
Camino for a couple of weeks, and still had his full pilgrim
flexibility. He ate, then turned to the things Fred had salvaged
from the wreck. He busied himself, clearing out his backpack
and his wife's, wondering what to do with her shoes, her
walking stick, things she'd packed herself that morning, but
would never touch again. He washed the dinner dishes, took
the pills the doctor had given him, scrubbed blood off his
shirt and shorts. He made telephone calls. He told his little
granddaughter what happened, but she didn´t understand.

His son headed out from Poitou to collect him.

The neighbors were upset we didn't share the news sooner.
Word didn't sweep over the village until much later, when the
car was hauled out of the field.

Oliva and Justi came over with the church keys, so Antoine could go there and pray if he wanted to. Remedios brought a vat of garlic soup. Carlos volunteered to drive Antoine to Palencia in the morning for his 11:30 appointment at the mortuary. Antoine didn't have a car, he didn't know the way. He couldn't think clearly yet, but he spoke good Spanish. Carlos said he'd take care of things. He'd be sure the funeral people didn't take advantage.

I walked him to the gate.

"I can't imagine," he said. "To suffer such a loss, in a land that's not your country, in another language. The poor man."

Over at the plaza, the party went on. The music bounced off the Peaceable's face, singing "Tonight's gonna be a good good night!" But that year we didn't dance. We didn't want to leave Antoine alone.

He went to sleep. He would be alright, once his son arrived, once he got home.

Antoine took his things with him to Palencia the following morning, and we did not see him again. He sent a letter at Christmas, addressed to the entire town, saying thank-you.

I told my friend Rafferty what had happened. He put Amelie's name on an official list of pilgrims who died on the Way. They said a Mass for her soul in Santiago de Compostela, on the high altar of the cathedral.

Antoine left his wife's staff behind. He asked me to take it with me on my next trek to Santiago, so I did.

Several pilgrims die each year along the Way. Thousands of people set out, and not all are prepared for the cardiovascular challenge, the germs, or the traffic. Part of hospitalero training is what to do when a pilgrim does not wake up in the morning.

That's never happened to us, in all our years of hosting. Amelie's death was as close as we ever came to losing a pilgrim in our care.

I've taken plenty of pilgrims to the hospital, people who couldn't speak Spanish, or had broken bones, or were feverish to the point of stupidity.

One morning we found a man collapsed along the trail. I went for the car, and some passing pilgrims helped me put the man inside. He assured them he was OK, that I was a taxi he had summoned.

I drove him to the emergency clinic in Sahagun. He spoke Swiss German, and he smelled like fever. He didn't make much sense. He asked me if I was a hippie. I told him No. He asked if I was a police officer, if he was under arrest. I said no. He asked where we were going, I said that he was ill, that he needed to see a doctor.

"I did not call for an ambulance. I don't believe you're a

doctor," he said anxiously.

"This is not an ambulance. I'm not a doctor. I'm just dropping you off at the medical center," I told him. My rusty high-school German was not up to this.

"You're not an ambulance. You're not a taxi. Why'd you pick me up?" he asked. "Why are you doing this?"

It was a good question. I pondered for a minute. "For the love of God," I said.

The guy went quiet. Maybe he's finally shut up, I thought.

"Jesus Christ," the guy said. "Another religious nut. You people are everywhere."

I looked at him. He was shivering.

"Du bist wirklich krank, mann," I told him. "You're really sick, guy. But you can walk the rest of the way if you want."

He let me bring him into the clinic, we found his medical ID, he settled into a chair. I told the attendant I'd found this man along the trail, and then I left him there with his backpack. We said no more to one another. I don't know what happened to him after that. What an ass.

See? I am not so saintly.

Some people should not walk the Camino. It is not for everyone.

Conversely, some people really should do it, and don't. Or they just can't.

Miguel Angel, for instance – he's a dear friend. He came to visit that summer, and fell in love with the Meseta. Miguel Angel lives in Paris, but he's from a little town outside Mexico City. He's right at home out here in the parched plain, where ladies called "Miracle" and "Remedy" serve up plates of pig ears and tripe and tiny songbirds.

Miguel Angel is a psychoanalyst, a healer of minds. He is a romantic. He was fascinated by the pilgrims he met at our house, he spent hours on the patio with them, talking about their homes and mothers and dark desires, what drove them to walk. He calls this place "The Golden Land."

Miguel Angel will never walk the Way because he was born with a twisted foot. He cannot walk very fast, or far. It occurred to me that Miguel Angel, a person I love like a brother, is one of those lovely spirits who need a little extra care. He is someone who ought to be wandering the Camino, healing and being healed, but who cannot.

Thunderstorms rumbled the nighttime, but the days were bright and hot. My new garden beds buried us in green beans and basil, but little else. The neighbors brought over boxes and baskets of grapes and quinces, figs, plums, apricots, and cherries. "Dessert," they said. "For the pilgrims."

21

FERTILIZER

September makes me sad. It's still green and bright, but the swallows fly away and the village empties out. The air is heavy with manure.

Once the sunflowers are cut, the farmers clear out the barns and stack mountains of dung on the fields. It stands out there for a long time, casting black shadows, until the tractors spread it over the field. The winter rain works it in.

Farmers who keep cows usually have manure spreaders, and a lagoon full of fully matured liquid dung. Those hardy souls drive up and down their furrows splattering a steady spray of fertilizer in their wake. It's efficient and uniform, and anyone within five kilometers knows what he's doing. An invisible cloud hangs in the air. It's a good day to head out to get some shopping done.

As owner of a new garden, I cast covetous eyes on the manure piles, the wagonloads rolling by behind tractors. I wondered where all that dung came from, what it might cost, how I might get some of my own. I asked Angela.

We sat on the church steps and we conjugated manure.

Estercolar, abonar, embonar, three verbs subtly shaded: muck-in, fertilize, enrich. Edu's cousin runs the dairy farm in Terradillos, Angela said. He supplies all the manure that Moratinos needs. I could ask Edu to bring me some.

We pulled closed the church door and walked over the street to Edu's house. We greeted Tina, Edu's 88-year-old mother, installed for the month in a lawn chair beneath the great fig tree. Angela shouted at Edu, and he nodded and shouted back. He wasn't wearing his hearing aid.

"I will bring some fertilizer for you," he assured me. "You brought me such a nice cake at Easter, I haven't found a way to thank you yet."

Cake at Easter? I thought. I didn't remember that. Oh well. I had about 12 zucchini squash in the house, all of them slated for zucchini bread. He might have even more cake before this was over. Over at the church four pilgrims were trying the door. We let them in. I ended up bringing them home. September of that Holy Year was non-stop, with at least two pilgrims every night, as well as several broken souls who stayed a while. Kim came back to help us, and we pushed her to capacity.

Una Dog developed a cough. She spent most of her time sleeping.

I coughed, too, and sneezed. The wind blew in the night,

and deposited a thin coat of golden dust on every surface, indoors and out. The sun was still summertime-strong, it baked the brown fields to powder. Every drop of sweat left a trail down our faces.

Late one morning I stepped out of the Bar Deportivo in Sahagun. Someone shouted my name from down the street. Shouting is not so usual here. I turned, everybody on the street turned, and from a block away a long, tall man came sweeping toward me, his arms open wide.

"Leo!" I yelled. He swept me up in a huge hug and kissed me square on the lips. This is how Leo says hello when he's not seen you in a while, at least if you are a woman. Men get a similar greeting, just not the lips part. Leo is funny and sparkly and utterly extrovert, a six-foot-tall Fred Astaire with a red do-rag on his head.

Leo was a gardener back home in Cuba, but the "Albergue On The Camino" dream took hold of him. He came to Moratinos in 2009, looking for a place of his own. He fell in love with the abandoned blue-door albergue site, which by then was for sale. He stayed with us for a couple of weeks while negotiating, measuring, and dreaming over what could be.

He couldn't make it happen, though. The bank said it was worth 30,000 euros. The owner wanted 80,000. Leo didn't have half that much, and the girlfriend who was bankrolling the operation got fed up and flounced back to Valencia. Leo stayed on.

Then Leo met Jema, a girl from Calzadilla de los Hermanillos, 20 kilometers west of here. They fell in love, so Leo went to live with her there. They opened a classy bed-and-breakfast inn, and all of Leo's dreams came true.

Leo still stops by Moratinos occasionally to leave advertising flyers, to coo over the dogs, to promise to trim the fruit trees (which he always kind-of forgets.) That day, Leo hustled me back inside the Deportivo. He bought me a drink and caught me up on things. "How is Patreek? The hens? Tim, and Una? How are you, my friend?" he chattered. There wasn't much time for me to answer. "What of Kim? What are you dreaming of these days?" he asked.

"Manure," I told him. "Abono. Fertilizer for my garden."

"Manure? You want manure? Get some sheep manure, it's totally the best for flowers," he said. "It's acid, so you lay it on now and let it rot over winter, and Voila! Flowers! Peas! Roses! Whatever! Better than cow manure, way better than pig."

"Sounds great," I told him, "but Justi sold off his sheep a couple of years ago. Nobody's got sheep around us, except the guys in Terradillos. And I don't know them well enough to ask them."

"You know me, Rebekah!" he exclaimed. "Jema's family has

hundreds of sheep, and the barn is bursting with shit! Come over and get as much as you want. I will help you move it!"

And so the next morning I gathered up a couple dozen big black rubber buckets and drove over to Leo's place. We loaded up our van with lovely, well-rotted sheep droppings. We shoveled and loaded for two solid hours, and didn't even make a dent in their supply. I drove home slowly with the windows wide open, so the flies wouldn't carry me away.

At home I put in another hour dumping the buckets one by one into the garden beds, front and back. Patrick raked it out, and the chickens leapt happily from one pile to the next, gobbling up grubs and bugs.

I scrubbed myself down in the shower, went to bed early, and slept the sleep of the righteous.

The following day was just as busy. I took the greyhound girls to the veterinary clinic at Leon University for their spay operations. We were there at 9 o'clock sharp, the church bells were ringing. After that I was free to wander the city until the doctor phoned.

This was a real treat – alone for hours, in a splendid little city! I had a big cup of coffee at the student cafeteria, and walked over the road to the library. A huge, wide-open library, plain red brick outside, but fabulous! I had not been inside a library for years, so I settled in and had a good two or three hours of communion with my neglected nerd side, scanning old property registers and architectural tomes, writing down new vocabulary words.

I got a little itchy, so I decided to take a walk in the sunshine. I hiked into the city center, up to the cathedral. Leon is not a big place, and a couple of years before I'd gotten to know its labyrinth of lanes while taking driving lessons for my Spanish driver´s license exam. (I'd been driving cars since age 17, but Spain doesn't recognize American licenses as legitimate. The examiner told me I am a fine driver, but much too courteous.)

I discovered a corner of the old city I'd never seen before, a section of the Roman wall, tucked alongside an ancient hospital. I treated myself to an Italian gelato, another thing never seen in Moratinos. I finished just in time to hear the bells clanging and banging, announcing the 1 p.m. service at the splendid Basilica of San Isidore. The place was packed. I wedged into a pew. My ankles itched, I wondered if there might be a late wave of mosquitos loose in there. Just when the priest raised up the sanctified host, my mobile phone went off. I dove for the door. It was the veterinarian. Come get the dogs before lunchtime, he said. All is well.

And right after that, a call from a group of Austrian pilgrims: They were on their way into Moratinos, and he wanted to reserve three single rooms with private baths. Ha!

I got back to my pew just in time for Communion, which was good timing – I'd missed church on Sunday. Then I hoofed it right back to the university.

The dogs were still groggy from the anesthesia, so they slept the whole way home in the back of the van. We learned very quickly their conical collars, designed to prevent them worrying the sutures on their bellies, were not designed for pin-headed dogs. Nabi slipped her head straight out of hers, and trotted around the patio waving it like a flag. We resorted to duct tape.

The house was full of pilgrims, and Patrick was kind to all of them. He spent the night in the storage room with the galgos, making sure they were OK, dosing them with medicines at the proper hours.

I woke up at 2 a.m., itching and scratching. I switched on the bedside lamp and realized the bed was hopping with fleas! My ankles were covered in bites. I must've brought them in on my pant legs and socks, I must've picked them up at the vet clinic, I thought. I went on a bug-spray rampage, I washed the bedding and my clothing in extra-hot water, took another shower, took an allergy pill, and went to sleep in the chemical-scented bed.

Morning showed the greyhounds, too, were scratching

and miserable. I combed them with a shedding blade and put fresh flea collars on them. We had company coming that day, and I had an hour or so before I had to pick them up at the train station. I went to sweep out the car.

The windows were rolled up tight, the sun beat down. I could see them inside the hot car, leaping like a cloud of acrobats under the Big Top: fleas. Hundreds of them! The car was infested! Where did they all come from?

I remembered Justi's barn in the spring, back when he kept sheep... you couldn't stand outside that barn without scratching. Fleas love sheep, and sheep barns. And sheep droppings. No wonder my ankles itched! I'd brought home a million fleas from Leo's barn.

I found the flea spray, opened the rear hatch of the car, and let fly until the can was empty. I slammed shut the doors again, and left it there to cook for an hour or so.

The train was late, and a good thing. The poison worked. I vacuumed out the car, and drove into town flea-free.

Patrick slept out in the storage room again that night with Nabi and Lulu. They'd stopped scratching, and were well on their way to health. I was spotted and scratching for the next week.

Fleas never bite Patrick. Mosquitos leave him alone. Life is unfair.

22

DOG PARTY

Una was a bad dog, a scruffy, selfish cur who'd steal the candy from a baby's hand, or empty the trash during the night to liberate the pork bones at the bottom of the bin. She didn't mean to be bad. She just knew what she wanted.

She liked to play. Her idea of play was rolling on the living room floor in front of the fire, growling and snapping while I hunkered down next to her, growling and snapping and pretending to fight. It always ended up with me scratching her belly, but she couldn't just peacefully roll over and let me do that, like soft old Tim. She had to have her belly-rub on her terms. Her scary, violent, growly terms.

We called it a scruffle. She knew the word. She came over in the evening when I was working on something, and laid her chin on my knee. "Scruffle?" I'd say. And she'd growl. It was time.

When Una stopped scruffling, I felt the darkness coming. She lay on the living room floor panting instead. Getting up from there was not easy since her leg was amputated, and toward the end, when the time came to go outside for the night's final wee, I had to pick her up and carry her to the back door.

The veterinarian said time was running out. There was nothing to be done for her.

So while she still could walk and bark and enjoy herself, we threw a Dog Party.

We loaded all the dogs in the car and drove out to The Grand Canyon, Una's favorite place, a tract of scrubland near St. Nicolas that's full of rabbit holes and hiding places. We brought a doggie picnic of fried liver and pig ears and bologna. Patrick and I were there, and Kim, and Tim, Lulu and Nabi – their stitches removed, their spirits revived. We lifted Una out of the car, and the rest of the pack flowed out and over the gullies and scrub. We chased and played and scruffled and feasted, we paid extra attention to Una, who took it as her due. When she tired, we all went home. Kim made a film of it, with a Paul Simon "Hearts and Bones" soundtrack.

We bought a little olive tree, so when Una died we could plant it on her grave. We chose a spot inside the patio for her to lie.

We stayed busy, we didn't want to dwell on the inevitable. There was plenty to occupy us: the stove wouldn't work, the internet only worked sporadically. The concert series wound up and Fred went back to America for a while. And Edu, true to his word, rolled up and dumped a full tractor-trailer load of cow dung outside the back gate. I suddenly had more animal droppings than I'd ever dreamed of, and we spread them generously over all our parched and neglected greenery. Malin and David came over with their collie pup, and Tim did not approve. The Irishman called John Murphy – namesake of Murphy the cat, came and put to rights a long list of broken, clogged, and crooked things. Finally everyone went away again.

One afternoon Patrick and I went to San Nicolas, to the bar at La Barrunta, to sit down together – just us – over a gin and tonic. We lingered in their shady patio, and finally ambled on home.

The front gate was ajar, a package was just inside. The package man had left the gate open. The greyhounds were gone.

Patrick went into a lament. I took off 'round the outer walls, because Lulu likes to hunt for cats out back. I found her there, I brought her back. She shivered.

No sign of Nabi anywhere. We walked the town, we called for her, and I drove the car to the Promised Land and up and down the Camino. I did that every couple of hours, and no luck.

Patrick slept in the barn that night with Lulu and Tim.

In the morning Nabi still had not returned. I took out the car again. I found her.

From the bridge over the A-251 motorway I spotted her, sprawled on the concrete alongside the guardrail, at the foot of a huge rabbit warren.

"Oh, Nabi Dog," I said. I started to cry. I drove the car down the bumpy access road alongside the highway, on the wrong side of the fence. I got out and scrambled down close as I could go. It was her for sure.

God knows how she got over the fences and onto that highway. I went home, I told Patrick. We had to drive down to the Ledigos interchange to get onto the westbound lane, had to pull up alongside and put on reflective jackets and shift her leggy body onto a sheet, and shift that between us into the hatch. I did all that with big fat tears streaking my face, asking her why, but she was way beyond hearing me.

Her neck was broken. There were no marks on her. She was stretched out full-length, a hillside of rabbits within snapping distance. We buried her out back. Una, Tim, and Murphy cat sniffed the body, then stood by and watched us move the dirt. Lulu stayed in the barn, whining in the dark. She knew.

The highway gave her to us. The highway took her back. Nabi was a wild dog, neurotic, a hunter to her bones. She was not meant to be a pet, but she loved Lulu and Kim. In her short life she'd learned to trust us.

Remedios said it was a shame. We'd just paid all that money for her operation, and there she is, dead! Maribel said galgos don't belong in towns, but then Maribel had lost a hen to Nabi's insatiable hunting drive.

Patrick was very silent. Patrick hurts plenty, but he doesn't know how to cry.

The weather broke, the rain arrived. I wrote a guide to the Camino de Invierno, and sent it off to the publisher. I translated my zucchini bread recipe for Remedios. The dogs hunted mice in the muddy fields. With her mate gone, Lulu regressed to her old scaredy self for a while. We woke in the mornings to fog, the fog that falls each night from autumn right through mid-January.

In early October the town filled up again for the national El Pilar holiday. The Segundino family picked the grapes in the vineyard, and stomped them into juice at their bodega. After church on Sunday everyone packed into the newly renovated "Local," a little meeting room in the town hall. We drank white wine and vermouth, everyone brought tortilla or pickles or olives and talked very loudly.

Keys were produced, and the church was swept and scrubbed. The cemetery walls got a coat of whitewash, weeds were sickled, and last year's plastic flowers cleared away.

We ladies stepped out in the evenings. I wore hiking shoes and carried a staff, but they walked in their house slippers, carrying scissors and sickles and baskets in case we found snails or mushrooms or alfalfa growing along the way. Remedios' sister Mariluz knows which mushrooms are good and which will kill you. Pin loves snails, he's the only one who'll take the trouble to soak them for days and salt them the right way.

On these walks I learned who owns which field, and where the monastery probably stood, who knows how many years ago – the plow still turns up tiles and shards there sometimes. I saw where the ladies washed the laundry back before washing machines, down along the creek where we'd built the labyrinth.

Angela told me about her new boyfriend from Zamora, and her new crop of students – Moroccan kids, Bulgarians, kids who already spoke two languages, and now were adding English. Angela had been offered a better post closer to home, but she loved these kids, she said – she opted to stay put in Salas for at least another year. She got permission from the principal for me to come again and speak "real Bart Simpson English" to her classes.

Pilar gave us apples. We peeled and sliced and froze them. We did the same with ten pounds of red peppers, bought for a song at the Saturday market. The trees turned yellow, and a big rainstorm brought down most of the leaves. New floors went in at Bruno's albergue. Drillers sunk huge wells at the hostel site for geothermal heat. They didn't fence the worksite. Pin's dog Braulio fell in and drowned.

We cleared the summertime plants off the patio and washed windows to a startling clarity. I pulled a Nine of Swords for my upcoming tarot card. The nightmare card, shocking sadness. Nabi. And Una, of course. Who needs mystical oracles when you've seen the X-rays?

A strange trio arrived on the trail, people who'd stopped before. Hermann and Hedda were Finnish evangelists. They ran an orphanage in Russia in summertime, and spent their winters sharing the Gospel on the Camino. They walked with Brandon, an American merchant seaman whose hitch had ended a few years before, in Malaga. He spent summers bumming on the beach in the south, and in winter he walked with the missionaries. They'd "led him to the Lord," and continued "discipling" him, he said. They were his spiritual parents, his stand-in mom and dad, the only family he had. He watched over them.

The couple had aged in the two years since we'd seen them. Hermann was 82, and this would be his final Camino, he said. He walked slowly, leaning hard on his stick. Hedda was still plump and spry, but her eyes were old. Brandon wore a bushy beard. His layers of clothes were tattered and gray.

He accepted a sweatshirt from the Lost and Found bin. They stayed for lunch. We loaded them down with boiled eggs, grapes, and mandarins. They blessed us and our house and animals, and walked on west.

Una followed me around the house through the days, yipping for attention. We'd agreed to have her put down when she was visibly suffering. But not yet. Each night when I carried her in my arms out to the back yard, she laid her head against my chest and sighed. Una took a long, long time to go.

23

GOODBYE

October went out with a bang, with a big feast in the plaza to welcome all the families home for All Saints' Day. There's a Mass for the dead in the church, and a procession out to the cemetery to bless the graves. It's a solemn time, but with a note of hysteria laid over – everybody's home, everyone's happy, these are the final days of sunshine, let's not waste a moment's time!

The sky was the color of lead along the horizons, but bright blue on top. The sun shone white, and empty branches threw long shadows. The men pulled out a barbecue grill made from a big water tank sawn in half. They filled it with dried grapevines, set it alight, laid a grill over top, and opened butcher-boxes of pork belly and lamb chops. They passed around a porron of wine, showed one another they still could pour a steady stream into their mouths from half a meter away. The ladies laid old doors over trestles, taped paper over them, set them with chipped plates and cloudy glasses. The wind picked up the paper napkins and tossed them into the treetops.

We brought out our enameled tin plates and jelly jars, and set our places under the awning of the church porch. Una came along, bobbing under and around the barbecue, grabbing up scraps and scratches, getting in the way.

The church bell rang at 2 o'clock, calling the stragglers in to the feast. I collared Una to take her home, and as I rounded the corner behind the town hall I saw Pin and Segundino and Juan there with a skyrocket in a launcher and a lighted cigarette. My God, I thought – Una loathes those rockets, they frighten her like nothing else in the world, and here's one six feet away, ready to blow. I bent to pick her up in my arms, to shield her ears, and with a silvery sound the rocket shot upward. I closed my eyes and held the dog to me, but she knew the boom was next. Una shoved away from me and ran, fast as three legs could go, hunkered low along the wall of Vitoriana's house, across the street, past the truck scales, out into the fields. The rocket boomed over our heads. A cheer went up.

I ran to the truck scale, over to the playground where the Camino recommences. Una was nowhere in sight.

We looked for her everywhere, even down in the ruined bodegas where the skyrockets sent her in the past, where the pilgrims go to shit. We looked in ditches, in the culverts along the Camino and the autopista, the Grand Canyon and Hare Field.

Una dog was gone.

There was no body to bury. We planted her olive tree in the plaza. For months we scanned the ditches and gullies of the Promised Land and tumberon, wondering if a scrap of wiry white might turn up in there, but it never did.

Una came to us out of the blue, on her terms. She left that way, too. After a while we saw the symmetry in it. She was dying anyway. It was time to go. She ran out of our lives with skyrockets and cheering in her ears, out into fields full of mice, just before winter turned the landscape to mud.

I contemplated the inevitability of suffering, and my great horror and resistance to it. I hate the suffering of innocents more than I hate anything in the world, and my hatred makes me suffer. Dying is hard work. Almost everyone has to do that job himself, for himself, on his own. My hanging-on couldn't keep Una from death, any more than my embrace could shield her from a rocket. I had to let her go.

I woke up many times in those nights, and looked to the sky from the tiny window by our bed. Up there to the south, cartwheeling over the faint lights of Villada, was Orion. His arms and legs straddle wide over light-years of space, his body splayed open to whatever comes, leaping, joyful, vulnerable.

November came. I had all the research done. I started writing a book.

24

SECOND CHANCE

Rain came, the sky came down and sat on the ground, we were fogged-in for days in a row. I poured myself into the book, I lived another person's story, a life lived a thousand years ago.

Patrick made vats of Bolognese sauce and served it up on spaghetti to wet wanderers.

Tim lay alone in his bed by the fire. He did not want to be petted. I took away Una's bed. Lulu stayed alone in the barn. She cried at night. We wondered if she was cold, or lonely. We were back down to two dogs. A lot less mess to clear up, we told one another. Much fewer worries.

I swept up mud, I mopped up footprints on the tiles. I was erasing Una. Every day she disappeared a little more.

She had to be dead now. I wondered where her body was. In water, in a ditch, turning into water? Or maybe lying on the earth, turning black, turning into earth. I wondered if foxes and birds had scattered her, so she'd disappear more quickly. I wanted her to become earth and water and air. I wanted her suffering to be finished, and peace to rest on her. I wondered about assumption, if maybe she'd barked out some mystical chord and was taken bodily away into the skies, like Elijah.

All this for a dog, I know! Ridiculous! Angela said she understood. When Tigretona vanished and left her with four tiny kittens to raise by hand, how she'd cried! But the kittens thrived. They were scrawny, but tough as shoe-leather now. We still had Tim, and Lulu and Murphy. "You have to be thankful for what remains," Angela said.

We did hopeful things. I planted bulbs in the garden for spring flowers. We drove to Valladolid to see the Contemporary Art Museum, a done-over Renaissance palace packed to the walls with postmodern bunkum. I invited my sisters to come and visit me in the spring. Patrick and I pored over the Daily Racing Form online, and made our picks for the big Breeder's Cup horse races.

Kim came back on a Monday morning with a new German boyfriend. It rained hard. When the sun broke through I trimmed the pine trees out back.

I was putting the dishes away when I heard someone banging on the front door. It was Fran, frantic, shouting. "Come now, right away!" he said. "Maribel needs you!"

Nobody in this town ever needed me. This must be serious. I told Patrick I was going.

I followed Fran down the street at a half-run, over to the

plain red-brick house, through the plain wooden door, shoes off. Into the pristine little sitting room so warm from the straw burning below the floor. Fran sat down at the card table, opened a magazine, and opened his box of checkers.

Something was very wrong. Maribel was there, bent halfway over, screaming. Oliva was there alongside her, looking wide-eyed and helpless.

"What is happening? What's wrong, Maribel?" The sound started to bend strangely around us, as if we were under water. I looked at Oliva. "Is she ill?" I touched Maribel, I bent to look at her, I wondered if she'd fallen, broken a bone, maybe having a seizure. Her body shook under my hand.

"Where is my mobile phone? Who should I call?" I wondered. "Where's Pablo? Is Pablo in the fields?"

Maribel straightened and looked at me, her hands were claws alongside her red face.

"It's my Angela, our Angela," she wailed. "The Guardia just were here. They told us she's dead."

"Angela? No," I said. "No." I felt very cold.

"Angela is dead. Your friend. A truck, on the road from Burgos to Salas." Maribel couldn't say any more. Her words were going wobbly.

"A couple of hours ago. Head-on, a truck," Oliva whispered. "I saw the police car and came over. Edu's taken Pablo to

Burgos. To identify her. To sign papers. Pablo called the other children and told them. They´re coming now. We are staying here with her until they arrive."

"No." I said. This was a dream, a nightmare concocted from all the sad things that had been happening. "No puede ser." This can't be.

Oliva pursed her lips and shook her head. A tear escaped her eye and squirted out onto her sweater. She watched me carefully.

"Sit down, Rebekah," she said. "We need to be here for a while."

The floor was hot underfoot, but I shivered. I pulled a packet of tissues out of the crack between the sofa cushions. Angela had put them there, just yesterday. She had a cold, I'd seen her tuck them in there... I gave one to Maribel. Her nose was running. She hadn't stopped wailing.

"Oh, my God. Oh, what a blow. My Angela," she cried. I started to feel myself sliding, started to feel sounds forming in my chest. I wanted to cry out, too, but didn't know if that was done, I didn't know how to behave, how to feel this.

I should let her mother do the wailing, I thought – Angela's just your friend, Reb, not your daughter. She's just the only friend you really have here, the only real Spanish friend you have. Just Angela. Just little Angela. And I started crying then, and I cried for what seemed like hours, in an ugly and unseemly way, but I couldn't really get hold of myself, even when Manolo and Feliciano, Pin and Juan came in the door and embraced Maribel. They cried, too, like babies, even when Don Santiago came in to pray with us. Pilar came with a jar of coffee so hot it burned my tongue. Fran sat mumbling in the midst of it all, arranging plastic checkers on the open pages of his magazine, neat rows, black and red.

Whenever the door opened we could feel the cold across our ankles, and hear the rain and the church bells. Both bells, in the cadence that tells the town that someone is dead. Man or woman. How many years old. Over and over, ringing over the fields, telling Terradillos and San Nicolas the news.

The coffee brought me back. I sat up on the divan, I felt the front door open again the draft flow over us, I saw Angela's beautiful sister Christy sweep in, her face blotchy. She embraced her mother, they keened together. Christy stood upright then and scanned the red, familiar faces in the room. She stepped over to Fran, and in one wide sweep of her hand his magazine and checkers exploded off the tabletop and over the room.

"No!" Christy screamed. Maribel stood up and took her daughter in her arms, and pulled her into her biggest embrace. They laid their faces against one another and sobbed.

And so did I. I cried, and I still cry, and as I write this years later I weep, because it still hurts me so deeply. People kept coming and leaving, and finally, once Pablo and Edu came back from Burgos, I left, too.

It was afternoon in the silent street. The bells had ceased. Rain streamed down. I was wearing new wool slippers, I hoped the rain wouldn't ruin them. I walked home to a normal wet November Monday, and told Patrick that Little Angela was dead.

In the gloaming I went with Kim and Uwe out to the labyrinth. We raked up the leaves, reset some of the stones. It needed to be done.

Patrick sat in the barn with Lulu. He stayed out there right into the night. He didn't want any dinner.

Funeral bells. Drawn faces. Bourbon and beer. Two days later a coffin floated light on the shoulders of weeping farmers up to the cemetery, into the family tomb. We said a rosary for Angela's soul, words of comfort for the hour of our death. The town was packed with people Angela had worked with years before at the autopista gas station, policemen, schoolmates, and that boyfriend from Zamora, looking stunned and ill. The funeral seemed to have little to do with Angela, who'd stood alongside us in the cemetery a few days before for All Saints. All the graves were still decked with fresh flowers.

A school bus brought Angela's students over from Salas. Tomas and Stefania, two of the brightest, remembered me from the raucous school visit the previous autumn. They shook my hand and said hello, and I walked with them back into town. The school was having a hard time finding a replacement for Angela, they said. No one wanted to come to Salas to teach them. They didn't want another teacher, anyway.

The children laid a wreath on the tomb. They gave a stack of their drawings to Maribel and Christy, photos of them all with Angela on school trips, in the classroom, making rabbit-ears behind her head. Everyone wanted to show me news clippings, to talk about how the accident happened, wondering why she'd crossed the center line in broad daylight, how that could've been. They had accident photos. I said no, thank you.

"Pray for her soul. It's November. It counts double," one of her relatives told me. "Angela died without the final sacraments, so she'll need lots of prayers. Rosaries, even."

That annoyed me. "She wasn't a sinner," I said.

"We all are sinners," the lady said.

The sun came out. Patrick and I took a long drive, out beyond Villada, into the plains, down a forgotten road to Villacreces, a ghost town that's melting silently into the earth. I was numb, only halfway there. We walked among the ruins, marveled at how this could happen to a town, conjectured on what keeps a place alive, and what condemns it to this. I wondered if Moratinos would look this way in fifty years.

Patrick said no. "Moratinos has the Camino," he said.

Something occurred to me.

The Road to Santiago runs through our town. It's not just a footpath, it's a second chance. And in 2010, a Holy Year, a pilgrimage earns a Plenary Indulgence.

A day or two later, once things settled down a little, I told Maribel and Pablo I had made a solemn vow. Before the year ended, I would make a second pilgrimage to Santiago de Compostela. I would do it for the sake of Angela's soul, so she could be freed from Purgatory and rest in peace.

A little glimmer appeared in their heavy faces.

"It's a holy year," Pablo said.

"But you already walked the camino this year," Maribel said.

"I walked for me. This one I can do for Angela. Only the last 100 kilometers. Only enough for the indulgence. I am still fit. There's still time."

I don't remember what they said after that. I finished my coffee and went home.

I don't believe in indulgences or purgatory. I am not even sure about heaven. I don't spend a lot of time thinking about eternity. Creation and Big Bangs and raptures and End

Times? Boring. No one knows. No one can know.

I go to a Catholic church every week. I am a part of a very Catholic pilgrimage trail, and I believe very much in the enlightening power of a good long walk. But I don't believe a pilgrimage can save your soul. Only God can do that.

I believe God doesn't give a damn about all the miles we walk and prayers we say and Scriptures we memorize. We do those things for ourselves, to draw near to God, but we don't get extra points for particular kinds of sacrifices. We benefit from spiritual discipline, but it doesn't make God love us any more than he does already. God loves us, period. If we walk his Way, and do right, and say we're sorry when we do wrong, we can live and die in peace.

Or so I thought.

Having Angela snatched away so suddenly, and seeing her parents suffer, made me put aside my own beliefs for a little while. I slipped very comfortably into a Catholic view of death and repentance, grace and redemption.

Catholics have death and damnation all figured out. Ideally, when you know you're dying, your family calls a priest to your bedside. You make a final confession and the priest prays forgiveness onto your soul. He then anoints your body with oil, a sign of the Holy Spirit, a reassurance of your chosen state. You can then die in peace, knowing your sins are forgiven.

But if, like Angela, you die suddenly, without a priest, you step into eternity with sin on your soul – maybe not mortal sins that would send you to Hell, but the white lies and selfish habits that take a few centuries of Purgatory to burn away. All is not lost, however: a dead soul's Purgatorial sentence is shortened when his friends and family pray for him, or they offer Masses in his memory, or do other penitential acts. Like, say, walking a pilgrimage.

And in a holy year, according to another scheme, if you walk the final 100 km to Santiago de Compostela, and confess your sins, and go to Mass, and pray for the pope, you get a Plenary Indulgence. Which means your purgatorial bill is paid up, and if you don't sin again you can join God and the saints in heaven. If you're already dead, and someone does those things in your name, you get full credit. It's a "get out of Purgatory free" card.

I asked Father Julio, a priest friend, if the indulgence would work for Angela if the pilgrim doing the walking was not a true believer.

"For God's sake," he said. "You're hurt, and you're helpless. Even if this Holy Year business is just a medieval superstition, it will bring her parents some comfort. It will open your heart to be healed. Go, go, go!"

Grace was right outside my door, rolling through

Moratinos and west. The Camino, and Catholic doctrine, was handing us a beautiful opportunity.

I had the time, but the clock was ticking. I decided to walk it as a spiritual exercise, for Advent. I would be outdoors, away from people, I could cry and not make everyone feel awkward, I could start healing my own broken heart. A plenary indulgence might put Maribel's Catholic heart at ease. A plenary indulgence was, for the next few weeks, within my reach.

I told Patrick I was going to walk for Angela.

"Why the hell not?" he said.

25

COMPANY

November moved on. Rom and Aideen, Irish friends, keepers of a pilgrim hostel in Moissac, came to visit. Pilgrims came too: a Korean called Son, and Jack, an Englishman who drank with Patrick and Rom into the night. They sang a song about a boat on a river, a haunting tune they all knew well, but I had never heard before. It was beautiful, rising up through the floorboards – one of those men knew how to harmonize. It was good, having a house full of merry souls, nice to do familiar things.

We cooked and cleaned, and commented on how much neater the house was without Una shedding white wiry hair onto everything. The weather turned wintery. I brought my photos of Angela over to Maribel's house, and there was a card from Rafferty in Santiago. It said a priest at the cathedral would say a Mass for Angela.

"Que guay," said Christy, Angela's sister. "Will you see Rafferty when you get to Santiago?"

"We can," Maribel said. She cocked an eyebrow at Christy, then turned to me. She put her hand on top of mine.

"Rebekah, I decided something," she said, almost in a whisper. "I thought to myself, I can't sit here by the fire, all nice and warm, while you are out there walking for Angela. It would just be wrong. I have always wanted to walk the Camino de Santiago. This is my chance. I won't let you walk alone. I will go with you."

My heart quailed. My God, I thought – this woman is in her 60s. I know she's a good walker, but 20-plus kilometers a day, for five days straight? What if she can't make it? And she loves to talk... Dear God. This could be a much bigger penance than I'd intended.

Maribel read the doubts on my face.

"Christy's done the Camino. She has all the equipment. You know I can walk really well. We don't have to be together all the time if you want to pray."

She had a train schedule marked-up already, and a calendar. We'd go on the 13th, she said. Santa Lucia. A growing quarter-moon, with Advent already underway.

It would be boring, I warned. I was going to take it slow, walking in silence in the mornings. I would stop at every crossing and chapel, and go to Mass every evening. The albergues would be cold, and sometimes noisy and dirty. I might not be good company.

Maribel sighed. "Rebekah, this is your promise. I respect

that," she said. "But you are doing this for my Angela. I am your support person. We're doing this together."

Jesus, I thought. What have I got myself into?

Moratinos closed in on itself. The doctor's weekly visit was where we all caught up on one another's lives. Toby Dog went missing for a week of romance with Flor's lap dog. They were spotted in the fields near Escobar, a good five miles away. Roldan, Juan's vicious German shepherd guard dog, was feeling sad, missing his friend Toby. Everyone was missing a dog, it seemed.

A big package arrived from America; a grateful pilgrim from the summer sent a deluxe dog bed for Una, made with suede and lambskin. Tim seized it for himself.

In the frosty, foggy mornings Tim and Lulu ran together along the creeks and hedges, hoping to flush out quail or hares. There were remarkably few animals out there, even though there are miles of open country and plenty of cover. I think, over the years, they've all been shot and eaten.

Lulu walked in the afternoons with me and Maribel – we did a six-mile loop to Terradillos, or a shorter one to San Nicolas, training for the hike to come. Maribel knew people in all the towns around us, and she stopped to chat with everyone, even when the wind was rising and the sun was setting. We sometimes came home in the dusk, with the streetlights juddering to life down Calle Ontanon.

The farmers turned the earth in their vegetable patches. Out in the vineyards they dug around the roots and twisted the vines together into long, pointy "alumbras." They look like Dali moustaches, or black tongues of flame. I took Maribel out on some of our old trails, over the Grand Canyon, past the beehives into San Nicolas. She'd lived in these villages for half a century, but she'd never been up there.

"There's a new world out here!" she enthused at me. "I feel like Christopher Columbus!" She let herself enjoy the open air, she let herself laugh. Back in town, where people watched, she and Pablo both kept straight, solemn faces. They could not be seen to be cheerful, not so soon.

In the Local I found an old group photo of school children lined up outside what's now the town hall. It dated to the 1950's, and showed our Moratinos patriarchs as very small children. I decided to frame it, and figure out a way to identify everyone, and put a key on the back. We could hang it in the old schoolroom where we met after Mass on Sundays.

I shopped at the big hypermarket in Leon for Thanksgiving, and won a promotional prize: a four-star *jamon*. The entire leg of a black-foot pig, a real treasure. I am not a big fan of Spanish ham. I had no idea what to do with it.

On Thanksgiving I made couscous and quails, green beans and biryani. Malin and David and Bruno came over. Antonio, the Portuguese "gentleman of the road," managed to hit it lucky, too. We had lots of food for everyone. We spoke in more-or-less Spanish, the only common language.

Bruno told us that Remedios' boys were turning their bodega – the big, deep one where we held meriendas – into a restaurant. Not great news for Bruno, nor the hostel. Three eateries in this tiny town, where presently there was none at all.

"The town is filling up with people," Malin said. "It's a renaissance."

"A very slow one," I said.

"Remedios says it's because of you," Bruno said to me and Patrick. "No one ever thought to invest in this place before you did it. Foreigners came before, but they didn't stay."

"We didn't open a business here," Patrick said. "It wasn't like we risked much... But then, I wouldn't open a business anywhere."

Bruno shrugged his big shoulders. "Santiago brings us here. Santiago will keep us."

On Sunday we took the jamon to the meeting room at the ayuntamiento, and learned that everyone has his own special method of carving a pig's leg. A special stand was produced to hold it in place, and Pablo produced a long, shiny *jamonero* knife. It's a man's job, evidently, and they took turns, peeling away layer after layer of fragrant, waxy fat until the deep red flesh finally appeared. It tasted to me like walnuts, but I was assured that's what an acorn tastes like. The black-foot pig eats only acorns, under the cork trees down in Extremadura.

The ham was declared "lujo." Luxurious.

It was a lujo gathering, a lucky day. We'd won the ham, and Pin had won a home-made salchichon sausage in a card game. The Segundino family brought pickled partridge eggs, speared on toothpicks with olives and anchovies. Arturo and Remedios unveiled a tray of langostinos. It was like a wedding reception, with no holiday at all on the calendar.

Snow fell outside the window; water ran down the pane inside. A bearded pilgrim knocked on the door, poked his head in, asked if there was a bar in town. Hands reached out for his coat, his bag, pulled him into the warmth, loaded a plate with delicacies. He smiled and waved his plastic glass of rough wine, and tasted a slice of jamon.

"Wow," he said. "Dehesa Calderon! Amazing!"

"You know jamons? You're from Extremadura?"

"Huelva," he said, "Next door to Extremadura."

"Is this ham genuine pata negra?" someone asked, "or is that pig wearing shoe polish?"

"This ham is better than pata negra," the guy said. "This pig had a better life than any of us. He died happy. You can taste it."

I rolled my eyes. The ham was one of the better ones, but it came from a supermarket. Still, I wasn't going to be an *aguasfiestas,* a party-pooper. The pilgrim was grateful, and thanked us with charming praise. When you're pulled out of the snow and into a party, a slab of boiled beef tastes like chateaubriand.

26

PABLO TOO

Back at our house, Patrick stripped clean the kitchen table and laid out a board of plywood. He took a big roll of brown Kraft paper and glue and shellac, and made a wonderful wrinkly brown thing, a landscape. It wasn't a painting, and it wasn't a sculpture. The room filled up with fumes, but no one complained. If we want to make art on the kitchen table, that's what we do. We're retired.

Three pilgrims arrived: a Pole, a Frenchman, and a Mexican-American. They'd overshot Terradillos somehow. We put them in the chilly salon and started some lentils cooking. Another knock came on the gate, another great ruckus of barking dogs: it was Milo, the Czech art historian who'd helped us out three years before. I'd only mentioned him the day before, wondering where he'd ended up.

He'd been busking in Santiago for the past five months, and was now walking slowly home. His hair was a nest of failed dreadlocks, his clothes were ragged, his boots flapped off the front of his enormous feet. He'd become a cartoon hobo.

He apparently had not stopped smiling in all that time.

We brought him in, put him in the single room upstairs, put his clothes in the machine and him in the shower. Through the evening he wore Patrick's fat green dressing gown and a pair of woolly socks, and he entertained us all playing "House of the Rising Sun" and "Heaven's Door" on the guitar, with kazoo accompaniment.

Milo showed the French guy the opening riff and chords to "Wish You Were Here." We wound up with a merry sing-along to "Everybody Must Get Stoned." Even dour old Patrick sang and clapped along.

Milo stayed a while, and chopped a winter's worth of firewood to fit the little woodstove. We found him some new boots, but he didn't seem to like them. He spent evenings in his room, strumming the guitar and yodeling his way through tunes he did not know.

He came with us the next Sunday to the after-church Vermut, where the snacks were all the trimmings from the Segundinos' matanza: jijas (the meat that goes inside the chorizos), crunchy fried pork rinds, quivering black cubes of fried blood. Remedios set aside the fried kidneys for Patrick. Milo was a vegetarian when he passed our way the first time, but he'd given that up, he said.

"For Lent?" I asked.

"No. For hunger," he answered, smiling his great smile.

Pablo and Maribel didn't go to the Vermuts. No one observed formal mourning any more, not even in Moratinos, but it just didn't feel right to go to parties yet, Maribel said. I stopped over on my way home, as I often did on Sunday afternoons. Maribel was napping, but Pablo brought me inside. He sat me down and gave me a cookie.

"A decision has been made," he said.

"I feel it is not right for two women to walk out there alone, especially this time of year," he said.

Oh no, I thought. He wants to pull the plug on us!

"So I am going with the car, with you and Maribel. You need not carry backpacks. I will meet you along the way, bring some food and picnics. I will find places to stay at night, inexpensive places. If something goes wrong, I'll be there with the car. So you can do this with no worries."

I thanked him. I left a handful of pork rinds on a napkin for Fran, and took the long way home.

My solitary pilgrimage of redemption was turning into a family tour. I wouldn't have any peaceful, quiet solitude. And with Pablo's reputation for penny-pinching, we'd likely sleep in truck-stops well off the route. My noble pilgrimage was fading away.

I asked God what he was up to, what he was doing to me.

He answered in his still, small voice: "Darling, this is not your Camino."

211

27

THE BREAKS

We rolled up to our little white graveyard with a wheelbarrow and some tools, and set to work clearing away the blackened flowers and wreaths still heaped on the marble slab.

It was the 8th of December, a month since Angela died. Christy and I cried, but no one else did. Fran said out loud what I could not. "Angela's inside there, but I don't believe it."

They said when Patrick and I die we can be buried in that cemetery, since we are now a part of the town. I know Patrick, heathen that he is, wants to have his ashes scattered up at the tumberon. I kind-of want to send my ashes back home to Pennsylvania, to Stitt's Run Burial Ground, where my settler ancestors lie. I do not think I will care, once I am gone. I don't care much even now, because I still somehow believe I will live forever.

Mid-December brings a meteor shower in Gemini. I had my telescope out for three nights, but saw no falling stars in there. Just naked-eye was enough to see them streak and shimmer. The crescent moon was beautiful enough to make me cry.

I got tired of crying so much, tired of waiting to go – the weather was beautiful for walking. Kim was already out on the Camino, sending back reports on trail conditions, leaving her little encouraging signboards along the Way for pilgrims to find. If it had been just me, I'd have started that week, but Pablo had some business to finish. Maribel said her bag was packed, we'd go soon as possible. I made up two credentials, and stamped ours with the Moratinos sello.

And finally, on Monday morning, we climbed into the little car and drove to Sarria, the starting-place for people who want to do the minimal mileage. We walked around the town in the rain, and checked into a grim concrete hostel.

Evening Mass happened in a stone-cold monastery up on top the town. We were the only laypeople there, our breath visible in the yellow candle light. A gnarled priest shook our hands afterward by the door. He listened patiently while Maribel told the story of why this pilgrimage was exceptional. She asked him to bless us.

The wind picked up, it blew cold under the great wooden doors. The priest put a hand on Maribel's head, and reached with the other to the holy water stoup. He put a big holy-water cross on her forehead, and her palms, too. And then he turned and did the same to me.

I am not sure if he blessed Pablo. I was busy hugging

Maribel, who was delighted. "We're authentic now, Rebekah!" she whispered, before putting her serious face back on.

In the church in Sarria I thought of Eric and Karsten, the two German boys who sacrificed their speedy, shiny Camino trip to help a sick woman get to the end of the road. I lit three candles, one for each of them. I wondered if Norma was alive.

I lit a candle for us three, too. Me, Pablo, and Maribel. I asked Angela to come along with us, if she could. If she wanted to. No worries now about endurance.

In the park on the way back, Pablo and Maribel asked me not to write about them on my blog. People might think they're "out on a spree" when they ought to be home in mourning.

Sarria is a market town much like Sahagun, but it has a peculiar buzz of its own. It's saturated with pilgrim energy. It's been a pilgrim town for ever, host to millions of travelers over hundreds of years, each of them with his own reason for being there. When we joined the pilgrimage, we stepped into a lineage that stretches back a thousand years or more. Nobody knew if we were doctors or lawyers or housewives, if we had raised the First Class Laying Hen or won a Pulitzer. We became just pilgrims, like all the other pilgrims there.

The Camino is "liminal space," set apart from ordinary time and place. Strangers connect instantly. Little family groups form, intensely supportive and intimate. Differences are overlooked, stupidities forgiven. Everyone lives and sleeps and works together toward the same goal. For many people, the walk is a profound, life-changing experience. And at the end, the family dissolves. Everybody goes back home, slender and tan and a little broken-hearted.

Sarria makes me feel the great size of the Camino. It makes me think big thoughts, and realize how small I am, how invested I am in things that don't last. Losing Angela made me realize that life can be very short, and I must make the most of the time that remains.

Dawn, our first day out of Sarria, we left our backpacks with Pedro and took off along the trail through the woods along the railroad track. Maribel zoomed off ahead so I could start my rosary undisturbed. Up in the thick woods, shushing through the rug of fallen leaves, she fell in with a pair of 30-something women. They chattered merrily uphill and out of sight.

You'd be hard-pressed to get lost on the Camino from Sarria. It's not only blazoned every few meters with the ubiquitous yellow arrows, it's littered with empty water bottles, candy wrappers, toilet paper, and advertisements for inns and cafes in the towns ahead. The mud is pressed with the footprints and tire-treads of thousands. It's easy to fall into the sweet cadence of repeated prayers, recitations of praise and appeal.

Rosaries aren't just for Catholics, or even Christians. I have my own way of praying with one. The beads don't just stand for particular prayers. Each can also be a person, a need, an illness, an injustice, a thank-you. In a couple of miles of walking I can step through all my family, friends, conflicts, fears, hopes, expectations, and issues. I lay them all out in the bright light of God's will, and thus empty my mind of their endless distraction.

And after that, I got down to business. Out there beyond the noise, I heard everything around me – my footfalls, my breath, birdsong, falling oak leaves touching down. I heard my blood moving past my eardrums, and felt my fingers growing cold and large as the blood pooled in the tips. I felt my ankles flex and twist as I stepped over roots and loose stones. Somewhere beyond the woods was a road with cars on it. Somewhere behind me pilgrims laughed. A dog barked. A radio played Shakira, football scores, and the shipping news from Vigo.

I heard every sound, but I let them all slip by. My mind was not snagged. It rolled to its own rhythm, and I called up a song, a hymn this time, in keeping with the situation. From deep in my mental archive came a revival number I'd not thought of in years, but I'd loved it madly at age 10, standing in our pew at the First Church of the Nazarene of Bossier City, Louisiana.

He lives, he lives! Christ Jesus lives today
He walks with me and talks with me along life's narrow way!

He lives, he lives, salvation to impart (and right here the pianist, a skinny maiden lady called Miss Cantrell, swept her fingers up the piano in a fabulous Liberace run)

You ask me how I know he lives... He lives (another glissando up the keyboard)

Within

My heart!

We sang the knobs off that hymn, over and over, when the spirit fell down on us. Miss Cantrell bashed that piano half to dust on a good night. And the homely little girl in the fourth row never forgot. Forty years on, I know every word to every verse. I brought it over with me to this pilgrim path in Spain, a place those Nazarenes would call The Mission Field.

Up to a little stone chapel I walked. A man was selling drinks out there, the same man who sold drinks there in 2001, when I last passed by. It was only 10 a.m., but I bought a cola, the full-strength red can, at the full-strength pilgrim price of a Euro and a half. I sucked it down, put the can in the trash, and turned to find the next arrow. Then I stopped.

This is a church! Time to do my duty.

The place was locked, but there's often a window so you can see the dusty little glory inside. I hunkered there (this is no country for tall people) and peered at the overdressed little doll on the altar. I spoke to God Almighty.

"Lord, like I said before, this walk is about Angela. Please do right by her – if not for her sake, then for mine. Seeing as I'm your servant, and I came here to do this thing. Take note, God. It's for Angela, Lord, wherever she is on your radar."

Other pilgrims were waiting to peek into the window. I finished up.

"Here I am Lord, on the Camino," I told him. "Look at me. Watch me. For Angela. For Little Angela," I whispered.

And God said, "Yes. I know. This was my idea. Get on with it."

And so I walked. At crossroads now and then sat Pablo, with apples and pears and bottles of water from his stash in the trunk of the car. He spread a blanket on a bench, peeled the apples for us, he chopped them into slices with his little paring knife, which we plucked straight off the blade. Pablo is not a jolly man, but he obviously enjoyed caring for us.

Inez and Amparo, Maribel's new friends, worked together in sales at the Corte Ingles department store in Valladolid, a fine position for any respectable woman. Maribel's own daughter Christy spent a season working at the Corte Ingles in Leon, back before she became a teacher. Both ladies grew up in rural pueblos like ours: one in Cantabria, the other in the mountains above Leon. Inez had a handicapped brother, much like Fran. I thanked God for sending them, for their patience and laughter and kindness. They took a load off me.

But for the second day, after lunch, when the conversation moved round to Angela's accident. Spanish people love to discuss accidents of every kind, to analyze the angles of impact, the conditions of the road and vehicles, the people in the vehicles, and how it all ended up. Maribel told it all to us, every detail she knew, with almost clinical precision.

I had not heard much of this before. I'd avoided all such talk in the days after the accident. I didn't want to know, but there was no walking away from this. It was probably good for me to slice away whatever denial I might have held onto. Angela had gone to Burgos that morning to a medical lab, for a work-related blood test. She'd had no food since the night before, and they took a lot of blood. She was rushing to get back to work in Salas, on a twisty two-lane road in the rain. Maybe – no one could say for sure – she'd blacked-out. Maybe she fainted. Maybe she'd shifted her attention to the radio, or maybe her mobile phone rang. But for some reason her car crossed over the center line. A truck hauling a load of granite was coming in the other lane. Boom.

The truck driver wasn't hurt. Angela died instantly. Blunt force trauma. Her car was demolished, but the inside was immaculate. She kept that car clean, kept the oil changed and the wiper-blades sharp. She was a safe driver, if a little timid. She liked listening to Top 40 pop songs on the radio. On a long drive back from Zamora in that car I'd sung along to a catchy old Kurtis Blow rap from way back in my high school days. I tried translating it for her,

Brakes on a bus, brakes on a car
Breaks to make you a superstar
Breaks to win and breaks to lose
But these here breaks will rock your shoes
And these are the breaks!

It was too much word-play and wit, too much idiom. In Spanish it made no sense at all, and not a lot more in English, but it had us both singing and laughing, all the way past Valladolid.

It made no sense at all.

The ladies noticed I was weeping. They told me "tranquilo." Peace.

28

WHO'S A PILGRIM?

We marched on. Our lodgings were seedy, but better than albergues. There were not many other pilgrims on the road, so we soon met the few who were: a couple from France, who'd walked all the way from Vezelay. Three young Spanish men, various professions, out of work – two of them delighted to try out their English skills. A New Zealander with amazing rows of teeth, who drank often and heavily. A large, slow-moving man from Portugal.

They talked with us, they talked among themselves. They knew why we were walking.

In a pilgrim register in Triacastela I saw Kim's name. She was out there, someplace ahead of us.

Maribel's toes blistered. I told her about coating her feet with Vaseline in the mornings. Pablo went out to get her some. We met on the street, he showed me to the church. Mass at 8:30 p.m., he said. I had a nap, then went to the service. Pablo was there already. He'd saved me a place. Our pew was just over a heating grate, the best seats in the house. Two local ladies in the pew across the aisle gave us the stink-eye – we had taken their spot!

We rose early and walked with the dawn at our backs. It was odd, not carrying a backpack, but I appreciated the ease. I went slowly, and stopped frequently. I got to know the old stone crucifixes, the chapels, the churches. Fellow pilgrims pointed them out to me, so I wouldn't miss any. I kept to my promise. I prayed at every one, I stopped over and over, saw inside several, got some interesting stamps on my pilgrim credential card. All the religion began to pall, but I didn't stop. This wasn't about me, after all.

I was certainly not the first person to do the Camino this way. And the longer I went on, the more clear it became – these miles of trail were not just the Catholic Disneyland shown in postcards and documentaries. Galicia has it all: charming villages, green forests, ancient pavements, delicious wine, cheese, and spectacular gardens full of things to eat. The trail is fully outfitted for vacationers and holidaymakers. On my first hike through here I'd had a high old time with my new best friends.

This time I saw the path beneath the shiny plastic skin. Here was a road worn smooth by generations of faithful who traveled from church to church, cross to cross, prayer to prayer. They made the trail a sacred Way. I felt my journey sliding along well-worn grooves of grace and penitence.

Local Christians were moved to commission stone "cruceiros," wayside crucifixes. Sculptors of no small skill carved a broken-hearted mother holding the body of her son. They erected these naïve carvings atop columns of stone, to mark the Way, and to remind everyone who passed that they did not suffer alone, that even God must suffer.

In my life I have seen thousands of artworks. The anonymous, weather-beaten Pieta on the cruceiro of Ligonde is the most beautiful of them all.

I sat down under the big chestnut tree nearby. I took a deep breath and marveled at the mildness of the December weather, the clarity of the bright blue sky. I looked up at the cruceiro and wondered at how the landscape around it must have changed since it was set up. Who put it here, what promise was made, and when? Cruceiros stand at crossroads all over Galicia, not just along the Way to Santiago. But we pilgrims like to think the crosses, chapels, cherry trees and sunflowers were put here just for us. We are special, spiritually charged, set apart from the ordinary tractor-drivers and milk-maids who also pass this way. Not to mention the tourists.

As the Camino becomes more popular with tourists and sports-walkers, a minor culture war rages over who is a pilgrim and who is not.

People who walk all the way to Santiago from France or somewhere beyond are usually considered pilgrims, but people who skip past the boring bits on a bus or train are lightweights, sight-seers, tourists. "Real pilgrims" take the good with the bad, they accept whatever the trail throws at them. They're respectful, they carry their necessities and not an ounce more, in a bag strapped on their backs. They keep it simple, they don't take the easy, or posh alternative. Rain, blisters, fierce dogs, bedbugs, blinding heat or deep snow, they keep walking. They're vagabonds with a peculiar respectability, and a great deal of self-regard.

I had been one of those "uber pilgrims," hardcore and self-righteous. But not this trip. I was doing only the final 100 kilometers, with my bag in the back of Pablo's car.

Maribel loved doing "traditional pilgrim" things, so we'd agreed to meet in Melide for lunch at Casa Ezequiel. What was once a family-run truck-stop has morphed into a great pilgrim feed-barn, specializing in tender Gallego octopus. It's a fun place. Right by the front door husky women hook rubbery sea creatures up from the depths of a boiling cauldron. They cut the tentacles to bite-size with industrial scissors, arrange them on wooden platters, and sprinkle on some smoky paprika. Pilgrims, and everybody else, sit on long benches and share the table with anyone else who's there. They chat in their dozen different languages while they wait for their platter to land.

The place was rather quiet that mid-December afternoon. The lady nodded us toward a couple of pilgrims huddled at one end of a long table. Maribel and I poured out the first of our little jugs of rough wine and introduced ourselves to a German cardiologist and a dog-trainer from Ukraine. We reached down and loosened our boot laces. The pilgrims spoke English, so I translated for Maribel. She enjoyed meeting people from other lands, but she felt guilty when I had to translate. She was happy to see Inez and Amparo roll up. She jumped up and took their coats, settled them in near to her, where she could comfortably default to Castellano.

The other pilgrims trickled in. Two of the Spanish boys, and their Korean friend. A new pilgrim sat down across from us, a lean, lanky, bearded guy. He spoke Spanish with a thick accent. He said he'd started walking months before from his home down in Cuenca. This was his fourth Camino. We marveled at that, poured out wine and water, nibbled on olives and lettuce leaves, ordered more. We started feeling warm.

Oscar, one of the Spanish boys, turned to me, he asked me to say an American blessing over the meal. Everyone went quiet when I stood up. I started in Spanish, but Oscar said "No, no no! The original!! And so they got the same one my

Grandpa said before each meal, right up to the last day of his life:

Lord Jesus be our holy guest
Our morning joy, our evening rest.
And with our daily bread impart
Thy love and peace
In every heart.
Amen.

Almost everyone made a sign of the cross, which would have appalled my grandpa. The pilgrims grinned, and the blessings soon turned to toasts. Pablo came in to join us, he slid onto the bench at the end of the table and nodded and grinned at all the good greetings. The Spanish boys introduced Pablo to the new guy, who turned to him with an icy stare.

"I know who you are, Mister Peugeot," he said. "Tourigrino. Driving a car from Sarria along the pilgrim road. Carrying the bags of these tourists." He turned his haughty gaze on me and Maribel.

I felt myself go red. I saw the man flinch. Someone had just kicked him, hard, under the table. I think it was Inez, seated across from him.

Pablo took the insult the Castilian way. He snorted, his face turned pink, but he said nothing. He looked away, he sipped his wine. Everyone went very quiet. Everyone but Amparo, in her thick glasses and sensible department-store sweater. She stood up at the bench and leaned over her octopus, close as she could go to the man's face.

"You will shut up. Right now," she said. Her voice was low, but it punched out each word like a printed notice. "Egotist. You walked all this way. You're almost to Santiago, and you still have no idea what a pilgrim is."

She sat down hard.

No one raised by a Spanish mother, or educated by nuns, would ever mistake that tone. The man looked around him. Every face looked back at him with the same cold regard. I felt my heart thrumming with tribal unity.

Oscar stood up and laid a hand on the man's shoulder, leaned over to speak quietly in his ear. Another big plate of food arrived. The two men stepped out for a cigarette, or a bit of air, an explanation. Everyone took a deep breath, another sip of something. We talked about the next few kilometers, should we stop here, or walk on to the next town? Is it uphill?

We feasted on octopus, we drank wine, chased it all down with coffee. Me and Maribel strapped on our packs and tightened our shoe laces. I went to pay the bill. The lady wouldn't take my money.

"The man from Cuenca paid," the lady said. "He paid for everyone, the entire table. He says he is very ashamed, he asks your pardon."

Oscar had told him what everyone knew. We were a grieving family, walking for grace and healing. We might be slackers, but we were for damn sure pilgrims.

We didn't see the man again that day. We got to the next town, we found our rooms, we went to Mass. And the following morning, when Pablo opened the trunk to put our bags inside, there were three pilgrim backpacks already in there.

"I'm not a pilgrim, but I can help pilgrims," Pablo said. "I'm going the same places they are. I offered before to take their bags, but only this morning they said yes."

Pablo is not a twinkly guy, but that morning he came pretty close. "The red backpack," he said quietly. "It's come all the way from Cuenca."

29

WELL DONE

The sun blasted down through the oak and eucalyptus trees, the cold breeze made them moan and squeal. I caught up to Maribel. We walked together, silently, over muddy streams, alongside pastures. We stopped to talk to a man in coveralls and a woman in a pinafore, turning the soil in a tiny plot of ground.

"I'm a farmer, too!" Maribel said. They stopped for a moment, and Maribel asked why they were working the ground by hand. They leaned on their shovels.

"We can't turn the tractor around in here," the lady said. "You don't see big tractors in this neighborhood, because we all have tiny fields and steep banks."

Maribel told her about farming the meseta, the wide fields, and their John Deere tractor, her husband's pride and joy.

"A John Deere? Wow. You must be rich," the man remarked.

Maribel laughed out loud. "Big tractor, big fields. But poor, poor soil. Clay." She pushed a clod of black dirt with the toe of her boot. "You have the little fields, but your soil is beautiful, and it rains so much. Everything grows here."

"No one gets all the breaks," the lady said.

"That's a fact," Maribel said.

The couple had been to Santiago de Compostela many times, but they'd never walked there, never gone as pilgrims. "Hug the apostle for us," the man told us. "Buen Camino!"

Down a long hill, around a corner, into the trees. A waymark pointed the way. On top the little concrete pillar stood a wooden sign painted with blue letters. One of Kim's. "Ultreia, Maribel y Rebekah!" it said. "Onward!"

"Que original!" Maribel said. "They even spelled your name right!"

Maribel walked right past, as if this was just another permanent feature of the Camino. I snapped a photo. After a moment's hesitation, I took the little sign and stuck it in my shoulder bag. That Kim! What a sweetheart!

Rain pounded down. On the fifth day my old Mack the Knife blister reappeared. I told Maribel I had to slow down. The paved surfaces were getting to me.

Maribel was bemused. "You are the young one, the experienced pilgrim!" she said, grinning. "I am your support. You walk at your own speed. Me and Pablo will wait for you at Monte de Gozo," she said. "We're almost to Santiago, Rebekah!"

So the 60-something woman I thought might be a burden

left me in a cloud of dust.

I caught up. After what felt like ages, Pablo found us a place to spend the night, right on the edge of the city. I was on the brink of sleep when my telephone rang.

"I have someone you've got to meet," Kim said. I could hear the smile in her voice. "You're going to love her. She's the cutest little thing!"

Kim was in Arzua, or Pedrouzo – some town a day's walk before Santiago. Somehow I'd walked past her.

"I'll need your help tomorrow," she said, "after you've finished the walk and all the cathedral business. I'm kind-of stuck. I spent the rest of my money," she said.

"On what?" I said, taking the bait. I laid back on the pillow and closed my eyes. "Why not just tell me what's going on?"

"In the eucalyptus woods, I heard someone following me. I turned around and no one was there," she said. "Creeped me out. I stopped and waited. And she came out, finally, from the brush. A little dog. A little girl. With spots. All wiggly. She followed me the whole way here. Her leg's been broken. She's all ribs and bones, Reb, but she knows how to behave, she was someone's pet. That's why I took her to the vet, to see if she had a microchip, if she belongs to anyone. That's why I'm out of money. And she's so much like Una. I think Una sent her. Or Santiago. She is perfect for the Peaceable.

She belongs with you."

"Kim, I don't need another dog right now," I said.

I could hear Kim's crest falling.

"Just think about it, then. I'm staying here for a day or so. Call me tomorrow," she said.

Early the next day, and Maribel and I stomped into Santiago de Compostela and up to the big square and turned to see the great face of the cathedral. We opened our arms and felt real joy come up from our souls. We made it, hallelujah! We embraced, laughed, agreed to find Pablo in time for the noon pilgrim's Mass.

But first, we had some business to attend to. We scurried around the corner to the Cathedral Pilgrim Office, where we climbed a set of rickety, wide stairs and waited outside the venerable office with the French couple and the toothy man from New Zealand. One by one we stepped up to the desk, presented our pilgrim credentials, waited while the clerk scanned our sellos and stamps to ensure our authenticity. Maribel was shaking a little. She went first.

The clerk found Maribel's trip legitimate. She stamped Maribel's credential with the final cathedral seal, then pulled out a Compostela: a formal document printed on heavy paper that certifies the bearer is a Christian in good standing, and has made a pilgrimage in the name of Christ as a holy pilgrim. She wrote Maribel's Latinized name on the dotted line, signed, sealed, and handed it back with a smile of congratulations.

It's a very busy office. That Holy Year, 2010, it issued 272,412 Compostelas. Ours were among the last.

My turn came. I glanced to the left, and behind a desk sat Rafferty, my Scottish friend, a cathedral volunteer. He waved me over. He had a certificate already made up, with my name in Latin inscribed on the bottom, the date, and the all-important "Vicari Pro" written over: "In Place Of." There in the middle was Angela's name instead of mine. I felt myself choke up.

"Well done, Rebekah," John whispered in his Glasgow burr.

Downstairs in the street outside were Inez and Amparo, the New Zealand guy, Pablo and Maribel, showing one another their certificates. The scene suddenly felt very Hollywood. Everyone went quiet and stepped aside, and a sunbeam broke through the grey clouds and shone down on that street corner. Rafferty appeared in the doorway behind me. I handed the parchment to Pablo and Maribel, and said "This is for you. For Angela. Her Holy Year Compostela."

That was one of the best things I've ever done.

30

ROSIE

We visited the cathedral and fulfilled all the rituals there. Maribel and Pablo decided to drive on to Finisterre, the "end of the world," an alternative ending to the Camino de Santiago. I told them I'd find another way home. Our business finished, we parted with smiles. I sought out my friends in town and we gathered for lunch in a cafe.

Kim called. She still had the dog, and they were throwing her out of the garage where she was holed-up. I told her I'd come and get her. I told my lunch companions what was going on, wondering out loud what I should do next. And as friends do, they found a solution.

Ivar drove me to the airport, and talked to his friend at the car-rental desk. They cut me a deal. I drove the tiny car from the airport to Pedrouzo, where I picked up Kim and the little dog, which was crammed inside a little five-and-dime cage. Not a handsome creature. Bug-eyes. Cringing. Awful.

We drove the many hours home to Moratinos. We decided the squirmy critter was probably part Jack Russell, part Chihuahua. She was still a pup. Her broken leg was fresh, but healing well enough on its own she didn't need any splints.

By the time we arrived at home, her name was Rosie. For Rosalia de Castro, a poet and writer who came from the same part of Galicia.

There wasn't much of a welcome for us. A family of Korean pilgrims was packed into the salon, and Patrick was cooking and sweeping, trying to keep up. Fred sat at the kitchen table sipping red wine, holding forth on his latest project.

Rosie emerged from the little box bowing and scraping, making herself as small and friendly as possible, expecting to be kicked. Fred reached down to pet the dog, and she widdled on the tiles.

"What a worm! A worthless dog," he teased. Kim ran for the mop. Paddy picked up Rosie, who snuggled in close. "She's a beautiful dog," Paddy said. "She'll get comfortable. Someone's been mean to her. She'll just have to learn to trust us."

Tim took no notice of Rosie. Murphy cat kept well away. Lulu was tucked away in the barn. We'd have to be careful for a while, as Lulu often viewed small dogs as toys, or prey.

All five of the Korean children petted and adored her, and the smelly pup was in heaven. The family were evangelists, Paddy said. They were loaded down with free Bibles to give away to pilgrims, but they weren't finding many willing to add the weight to their backpacks.

The mother was in bad shape, Paddy said. He'd taken her to the doctor, and translated the proceedings to her husband, who spoke some English.

"Your wife is exhausted, ready to drop," Paddy had told him. "Here is a prescription for vitamin tonic. She must go to bed now, and stay there, total bed rest, for five days." The woman didn't understand any of this. Her husband had sat there, impassive.

"She can stay with us at our house, while you continue on with the children," Paddy said. "After five days we will bring her to wherever you are."

"No. We continue on the road tomorrow," the husband said. "She has a job to do. She has to walk."

"Then you must leave her share of the Bibles at our house," Paddy said. "We will give them to the pilgrims ourselves."

The arrival of Rosie enlivened the bored children. We gave her a bath, apparently a new experience. The little dog shrieked like a little girl, and the kids laughed out loud. It was odd music.

I didn't have much of an opinion about Rosie. I was exhausted. I went to bed.

In the morning the pilgrims left us. Paddy and I bowed our heads and the family surrounded us, laid their hands on our heads and shoulders, and each one prayed God's blessing onto us in thundering, simultaneous Korean.

Kim drove the little car all the way back to Santiago airport, and parked it in the rental lot only 22 minutes short of its 24-hour special-price limit. Her mission accomplished, she hitchhiked back to Pedrouzo. She walked on from there to Santiago, and on from there to the ocean at Finisterre.

Christmas was on its way. We cleaned up litter along our stretch of the Camino, put up some twinkly lights. Oliva gave us a bottle of homemade *anis,* the Segundinos gave us a fresh chorizo sausage. On Christmas day we roasted a capon.

The following evening, Remedios' family threw a tasting party. They lined up bottles of homemade "orujo," white lightning, each flavored with cherries, rosemary, peppermint, coffee beans, or saffron. Sampling them all was not for the faint-of-heart, or stomach. They spooned the macerated cherries over cookies, and soon everyone was laughing and shouting, their cheeks glowing brilliant red. Back at home, at almost midnight, Fred decided to bleed the trapped air from all the radiators in the house.

The new year came up fast. Patrick went to England to pass the holiday with his sons. I stayed behind. Fred stayed, too—he was supposed to go to the mountains, but the mountains were snowed-in. We sat up late to see in 2011. He brought some good Bordeaux.

I tried to get London on the computer, to hear them sing

in 2011. We settled on jazz from the public radio station in Pittsburgh. I felt a little homesick. I was glad Fred was there, with his flat Midwest accent and his wild stories, and little Rosie, too, curled up by the fire.

The night was dark and windy. Fred tuned the guitar. Out in the barn I heard Lulu bark. And from upstairs came a great thumping sound. Someone was pounding on my bedroom door, the unused door that leads out onto the N120. Maybe an accident? A robber? I jumped up, told Fred to come with me. We sprinted upstairs, down the corridor. I unlocked the door to the outer darkness.

It was a pilgrim, pale-faced with exhaustion.

"Help me," he said. "I'm a pilgrim. I am lost."

"There is a bed for you here," I told him. I took his arm, walked him through my room, down the hall, into the neat green bedroom. Fred took his backpack, took his coat. "There's the bathroom. Come downstairs, when you're ready for a glass of wine."

After a little while he came down, still looking stunned. He said thank you.

"You're English?" he asked. He was German, but spoke lovely English. "Yes," I told him. "Well, I am American."

"What is this place?" he said. "What are you doing here, in the middle of nowhere?"

the end.

EPILOGUE
2019

More and more I walk alone in the Promised Land. Patrick doesn't have the energy to go the whole way around. He walks with us down to The Swimming Hole, then he turns back for home.

The dogs go with me, onward, out to the ridge where the windmills wave their arms forever. Judy Dog, Ruby, and now a little black sheep-herding dog Paddy got for his last birthday. She is full of energy and intelligence. She worked for a shepherd, but was much more interested in people than sheep. The shepherd gave her to Kim. Kim gave her to Paddy. We named her Grace.

Kim doesn't stay with us now. She found her dream in Rabanal del Camino, a tiny pueblo on a mountain outside Astorga. She shimmers now at The Stone Boat, her own bed-and-breakfast inn. David the Dutchman helps at Stone Boat when something needs to be repaired. He still does painting at Peaceable, too. Jobs are hard to find in Spain, even for skilled workers. David traveled for three summers with a troupe of acrobats, rigging their trapezes. Last year he helped to sail a rich man's catamaran from Ibiza to the Canary Islands. He says he's going home soon to Holland.

Two years ago, beautiful Malin left David and their tiny camper home and started a new relationship. She lives in a stone house with her jolly Spanish partner and his three sons. She sings at open-mike nights at the blues bar in Castrillo de Polvazares, and drives to a string of rural villages to teach yoga classes. She has her own horse now, and a sheep, and three huge Mastiff dogs. And Bjork, the collie she shared with David.

Ryan is still at large, posting updates and photos on social media.

Maribel and Pablo are grandparents several times over. Fran lives in a care home in Villada, where he enjoys daily handcrafts and lots of company.

Unlike most Meseta villages, Moratinos is growing. Bruno's albergue is open in the summer, offering massages and chakra alignments along with spaghetti carbonara.

The Hostal Moratinos captures most of the pilgrim traffic, right at the entrance to town.

Carlos and Juan hollowed out two bodegas and opened up a white-tablecloth restaurant, which gives the town a bar to gather around after Mass on Sundays.

Pilgrim numbers are down on the Meseta. Fewer seem

willing to walk this difficult way. Our door is still open, but travelers only come to Peaceable in the wintertime, when everywhere else is closed, or when they don't have any money to pay for a room. Summertime pilgrims seem to prefer a business transaction over dinner with a family and a bed in the spare room. That's OK, most of the time. Pilgrims are a lot of work. We don't miss them very much. We have found other ways to serve on the Camino.

New people have moved into town, even a child lives here now. No one has died for a very long time.

It cannot last forever, but we hold steady, living for right now. We are privileged. Every morning I walk in the Promised Land with Ruby, Judy, and Grace.

ACKNOWLEDGEMENTS

Laurie Dennett, Filipe Branco Madeira, Kathy Gower, George Greenia, Mitch Weiss, Cyrus Copeland, John Rafferty, Beth Caporali, and a host of pilgrims never stopped asking when this book was going to happen. Some of them worked to find it a publisher, an agent, or a "real deal."

Kim Narenkivicius did the heavy lifting. She continues to flex her "freakish strength," even when the days are dark and hope seems far away. I dedicated this book to Paddy at her suggestion, but "Furnace" truly is Kim's book. If it is my baby, Kim is the midwife who brought it into the light and kept it breathing.

I owe much to Cora Scott Cole, my mother, a poet, writer, and "walking dictionary;" and my Grandpa Guy France, a storyteller sprung from a long line of tale-spinners. I tip my hat to Bob Martinson, wordsmith and editor extraordinaire at the Pittsburgh Post-Gazette; Sally Vallongo at the Toledo Blade; and Mitch Weiss, whose Pulitzer-winning prose still keeps my editing skills razor-sharp.

And to Moratinos, my heart's true home... I hope my "Valentine" does not get me driven out of town!

ABOUT THE AUTHOR

Rebekah Scott is an American journalist, book editor, and author who lives with her husband and many animals in northern Spain. She is founder and CEO of Peaceable Projects Inc., a US-based charity that funds and coordinates good works along the Camino de Santiago trail network. She is a novice in the New Benedictine Community, an order of dispersed Christian monastics. She has two adult children and a granddaughter in the United States, and a large step-family in England.

www.peaceablekingdomcamino.com

Made in the USA
Coppell, TX
14 December 2019